BECOMING A LEADER OF LEADERS

Becoming a Leader of Leaders: How to Succeed in Bigger Jobs and Still Have a Life
Copyright © 2022 by Ian Lees.
All rights reserved.

Grammar Factory Publishing
MacMillan Company Limited
25 Telegram Mews, 39th Floor, Suite 3906
Toronto, Ontario, Canada
M5V 3Z1

www.grammarfactory.com

Lees, Ian
Becoming a Leader of Leaders: How to Succeed in Bigger Jobs and Still Have a Life /
Ian Lees.

Paperback ISBN 978-1-98973-755-2
Hardcover ISBN 978-1-98973-757-6
eBook ISBN 978-1-98973-756-9

    1. BUS071000 BUSINESS & ECONOMICS / Leadership. 2. BUS030000 BUSINESS
& ECONOMICS / Human Resources & Personnel Management. 3. BUS012000 BUSI-
NESS & ECONOMICS / Careers / General.

Production Credits
Cover design by Designerbility
Interior layout design by Dania Zafar
Book production and editorial services by Grammar Factory Publishing

Grammar Factory's Carbon Neutral Publishing Commitment
From January 1st, 2020 onwards, Grammar Factory Publishing is proud to be neu-
tralizing the carbon footprint of all printed copies of its authors' books printed by or
ordered directly through Grammar Factory or its affiliated companies through the
purchase of Gold Standard-Certified International Offsets.

Disclaimer
The material in this publication is of the nature of general comment only and does
not represent professional advice. It is not intended to provide specific guidance for
particular circumstances, and it should not be relied on as the basis for any decision
to take action or not take action on any matter which it covers. Readers should obtain
professional advice where appropriate, before making any such decision. To the
maximum extent permitted by law, the author and publisher disclaim all responsibility
and liability to any person, arising directly or indirectly from any person taking or not
taking action based on the information in this publication.

BECOMING A LEADER OF LEADERS

HOW TO SUCCEED IN BIGGER JOBS AND STILL HAVE A LIFE

IAN LEES

Dedication

On Wednesday, 4 August 2021, my eldest child, Katie Lees, died at 34 years of age from the AstraZeneca COVID vaccine. Katie got the AstraZeneca vaccine because she cared deeply about people and communities and was concerned about the impact of COVID lockdowns on mental health and human relationships. She believed that the only way the lockdowns would stop was by everyone getting vaccinated. Katie's sacrifice, and those of many others who died as a result of COVID-19 and vaccine failures, did eventually lead to the ending of lockdowns. She'd be so happy to see everyone out and about again!

Katie was a vibrant, healthy young woman. She was a writer, performer and comedian who gave hope, joy and inspiration to everyone she met. She loved the colours of sunrise and sunset. At the time of her death and for many months after, literally hundreds of people described how Katie had inspired and motivated them to truly live and to pursue their deepest dreams and desires. I wish you could have met her.

This book is dedicated to Katie and the amazing short life she lived. The person Katie was, and the way she lived, is what finally gave me the courage and perspective to push forward with the publication of this book. I truly hope that this book and the spirit of Katie will inspire and encourage you to grow into a thriving, present and impactful leader of leaders.

'*Becoming a Leader of Leaders* is a brilliantly thoughtful read, filled with practical ideas and strategies that would help any leader navigate the daily struggle of trying to keep on top of it all.'

'Working in the field of leadership I have read about many models, theories and personal accounts of becoming a leader which promise to solve all your challenges. What makes this book distinct is that it combines empathy for the human experience of becoming a leader of leaders with deep theory and powerful self-reflection questions to take you on your own journey. Ian writes in his closing chapter that one of his most powerful insights is that "each one of us is a unique being", and while there is a lot to learn from collective wisdom, "we must find a way that works for us and is us". This book provides you with the tools and knowledge to do this.'

'This book is an important reminder that our ways of thinking and working may need fundamental shifts as we transition into larger and more complex leadership roles. As a handbook for change, this book provides aspiring and new leaders with essential guidance for navigating transitions.'

'This book will open your eyes to what success really looks and feels like in a senior leader role, [and is] a must-read for anyone taking the next step in their career. Easy to read, with practical tips you can start implementing straight away.'

Annika Haddock, Finance Leader, GenesisCare

'Ian has an incredible knack of making sense of what's going on both within organisations and within your own mind as a leader. He brings clarity without simplifying, and his advice is non-judgmental and grounded in reality. I started off my work with Ian as a complete cynic, doubting the premise and practice of "management training". After working with Ian for a year, I enjoyed my job more – and I know that my colleagues benefited from my fresh approach to leadership.

'Ian doesn't try to turn you into a cookie-cutter model of a perfect leader, but encourages you to develop your own personality and strengths so that you can be the best version of yourself in the context that your role requires. He moves easily between theory and practical application, drawing on wide experience but always engaged with the realities of your particular role. I never failed to leave my sessions with Ian feeling more empowered and optimistic about my role, and with a stronger sense of what I wanted to achieve and how to get there.'

Toby Chadd, Director of Artistic Planning, Australian Chamber Orchestra

'A survival guide and invaluable companion for new leaders of leaders.'

'It is great to see Ian sharing his lifetime of wisdom in a book. As a person who understands and reflects on leadership daily, Ian has set out in this practical book his insights into one of the toughest transitions in the workplace – from team leader to leader of leaders. How we make this transition when the opportunity arises affects every part of our life and every part of the organisation in which it happens. This primer can help each of us be more self-reflective and effective as we take on more responsibility.'

'*Becoming a Leader of Leaders* is a practical and insightful guide to navigating the complexity of leadership development. Ian brings experience and wisdom to define and coach us through the three stages of leadership. A must-read for anyone in a leadership role or who is trying to help develop themselves or others in the workplace. I wish I had read this book 25 years ago!'

Contents

About the author   1

Introduction   3

PART ONE: A TIME OF TRANSITION   **11**
   Chapter 1: Letting go of what used to work   13
   Chapter 2: From overworked to influential   33

PART TWO: MAKING THE CHANGE   **55**
   Chapter 3: Adapt your way-of-being   59
   Chapter 4: Give yourself a promotion   87
   Chapter 5: Create sandboxes for your leaders   105
   Chapter 6: Influence to integrate   127

Your new future   147

Connect with me   152

Acknowledgements   153

Further reading   156

About the author

Ian loves helping people grow into who they really want to be. He provides coaching programs that help people grow into bigger jobs and bigger lives, especially bigger leadership roles. Ian does this by helping people uncover ways-of-being that are constraining them and create new perspectives that foster growth towards who they really want to be. He draws on a wide range of traditions, disciplines, perspectives and experience that combine to give people coaching experiences that are profound and practical.

Ian works with leaders and other senior professionals who want to move into bigger jobs, and people who feel like their present life doesn't reflect their full potential. He has worked with senior, emerging, and high-potential leaders in large and complex organisations across the private sector, government and not-for-profits, including Insurance Australia Group, Thales Australia, NSW Health, Transport for NSW and UnitingCare.

Ian's broad and deep experience in coaching, leadership development, talent development and management is supported by qualifications that include a master's in human resource management and a graduate diploma in Ontological Coaching. He also holds accreditations in a wide range of leadership development tools, including the Leadership Circle, Human Synergistics Leadership Impact and Lifestyles Inventory, and the Myers–Briggs Type Indicator.

For Ian, the heart of leadership and leadership coaching is total respect for the value and giftedness of every individual. Human beings are way more complex than even our most clever theories about them can conceive, and the respect we pay each other must include honouring the learning and decision-making of the past. Ian serves his coaching clients best when he helps them to become better observers of themselves and the world, and by helping them to see other possibilities for growth and action. It is not about 'fixing' people – rather, Ian loves seeing people grow in their ability to observe themselves, take responsibility for what they can change, and develop the courage to do it.

More recently, *Becoming a Leader of Leaders* has been developed into a leadership development program, designed and delivered by Being Leaders (www.beingleaders.com.au). Based on practices in this book, Being Leaders has designed its program to provide tools and resources for people in leader-of-leader roles to be more effective and impactful.

Ian lives in the Blue Mountains west of Sydney, Australia.

Introduction

IT'S ONLY 9:30AM ON MONDAY AND AMANI IS ALREADY stressed out by the constant stream of emails, phone calls, meetings and the 'have-you-just-got-a-minute' conversations with her team leaders.

Amani had been so excited when she got the promotion from team leader of three analysts to manager of all four analyst teams. She thought this was her big career breakthrough. 'Wow,' she thought, 'I am the manager of a total team of more than thirty people!'

But one month in, Amani found herself dreading Monday mornings by 3pm on Sunday afternoons, when she was supposed to be relaxing with family and friends.

When Amani was leader of the analyst team, she felt confident, enjoyed her team and loved the work. She really enjoyed pulling together the insights that she could generate through her analytical skills and her deep knowledge of data and systems. But now, Amani's days and weeks feel chaotic and out of control.

Every day is a constant stream of questions, problems, people not getting on with each other, and team leaders that are paid nearly as much as she is who ask the same questions over and over again.

And then there are the meetings she must go to now: the senior leadership team meeting, the Culture Change Initiative meeting, the Innovation and Improvement Project meeting, and the Future of the Business planning sessions. Amani sits in these meetings listening to people drone on about hypothetical stuff that has nothing to do with getting the actual work done.

Amani's team leaders, who were so friendly to her on her first day, now sit in meetings looking at their phones with sullen expressions on their faces. When she requests information or asks a question, the response is deathly silence. So, Amani gives them the answer or just tells them what they should do because she can't stand the long, awkward pause. At 11pm each night, when she finally logs off, Amani sits in the silence of her now-dark home and wonders, 'What has happened?'

I'm betting that your experience in your first role leading leaders has more than a little resemblance to Amani's.

When you move into a position where you're leading other leaders for the first time, you are doing a totally different job from anything you have ever done before.

So how is it different? And what is a 'leader of leaders' anyway?

Here's some quick definitions so we know what we're talking about. There are three types of roles we will be discussing in this book:

Professional contributor is a role where you use your professional skills and knowledge to get work done – for example, a finance professional using their accounting knowledge to prepare and interpret a profit-and-loss statement.

Team leader is a role where you supervise and coordinate the work of other professional contributors. Usually, you become a team leader in a field where you have previously been a professional contributor, which is why, most often, you will continue to do your own professional contributor work in your new role. An example might be a team leader of a finance team who produces and interprets financial reports.

Leader of leaders is a role where you have multiple team leaders reporting to you. These team leaders typically manage three to ten professional contributors. You now have team leaders reporting to you who are focused on shaping results through their own leadership.

In this role, you may not actually do any professional contributor work anymore. You may not even have a background in the work your team leaders supervise. Team leaders lead other people, but leading other leaders is a totally different job. For example, a leader of leaders could be someone who runs a finance operations group. Under them, there are six team leaders supervising different aspects of the organisation's accounting and reporting systems.

Your new job has a much bigger span; there is a lot more going on. Often, people making this career change end up working ridiculously long hours. They get home, make dinner, eat, then log back on and keep going until 11pm, and sometimes later. They say to themselves, 'If I just work late tonight, I will get on top of everything.' But you never 'get on top of everything', and so your one night a week of working becomes two, and then three … you know exactly how it goes.

Is this your life? Take a moment to complete this checklist to see. Tick the statements that you can relate to:

☐ Even when you are not working, you are thinking about it. You get phone calls, text messages and emails at all hours, and you feel you must deal with them right then or they will just pile up.

☐ The leaders that report to you seem to be incompetent and incapable of solving problems, or even thinking much.

☐ The leaders that report to you are forever coming to you with problems in their teams and work they can't get done, and they seem to dump it on you to sort it out because you are the boss.

☐ There seems to be an endless stream of tasks to get done – often big ones that you never seem to get to, and they keep piling up.

☐ You feel like it's important for you to be fully across everything that your team is doing.

The problem is that you have moved into a completely different job, but you are still trying to do it using the mindset and work practices that you have learned in the past and that worked for you as a leader of individual contributors. Some of the skills you have developed in your previous role will be useful in your new role as a leader of leaders, especially people skills like coaching and giving feedback. But relying on these will not be enough to make the change.

If you keep doing your new leader-of-leaders role the same way you did your previous role, you will crash and burn.

The impact this may have on your career, your health and your life can be devastating.

But if you understand that being a leader of leaders is a totally different job, different from anything you have ever done before, then there are some important and powerful steps you can take to make meaningful changes in your life. Simply, you must unlearn what used to work for you and learn new work practices that will enable you to not just do this new, bigger job, but also flourish in it and open possibilities for greater impact, influence, job satisfaction and life balance. You can grow your role into healthy hard work, instead of soul-destroying busyness.

The ideas and practices in this book were born from working closely with ordinary people who are trying to make this big job change from team leader to leader of leaders.

In this book, I'll help you to understand why you are in this dilemma and how to get out of it. I'll introduce you to new ideas and practices that will guide you in your leadership development. I will show you how the way we think determines how we interpret what's going on around us, and what we see and believe to be possible. The leader-of-leaders role is all about constantly trying to make sense of what is going on, work out what is most important, and then determine actions within the range of what's possible.

Understanding how you think and adapting your perceptions is a core part of succeeding as a leader of leaders. From this foundational understanding and practice, you will be able to make the big changes in your work you need to succeed at this new and totally different job.

As you make the transition to your new job, and as you focus on your work and give more shape and structure to your role, you will start to feel the satisfaction in having a broader and bigger impact.

The approach and techniques in this book are practical and proven – deep and fundamental. There is no escaping the reality that being a leader of leaders is a demanding, complex, whole-person job. To do it successfully, you have to grow the core aspect of who you are as a person and how you see yourself in the world, so that you can act with decisiveness and confidence. Working on yourself from a deep and profound level will help you make practical and sustainable changes in how you act as a leader. The idea that all you need are some quick tips and tricks to achieve the results you want can be attractive, but it is also unrealistic. I'm sure you know your journey of becoming a leader of leaders is more complex and messier than that!

The full term 'leader of leaders' is really important because it captures a major transition in your career, but it can be a mouthful if you repeat it lots of times! So throughout the book, I'll sometimes refer to leaders of leaders as, simply, 'leaders', or 'senior leaders'.

Drawing on my long experience in coaching leaders, and my further studies in Ontological and Somatic coaching, this book will give you profound practices that will enable you to become a successful leader of leaders. And as you grow and develop new practices, the possibilities of succeeding in even bigger leadership roles in the future will open for you.

Are you ready?

PART ONE:

A TIME OF TRANSITION

Congratulations! If you are reading this then you have probably just been promoted, are about to be promoted, or are thinking you would like to be. The role you want is in a whole new world. It's a big step up with great opportunities, but this transition doesn't just happen. There are some traps along the way that can derail your transition, and even your career.

In Part One, we'll explore the ways you can get stuck. You'll discover how some of the work practices that made you successful as a leader of individuals can get in the way of you growing into a leader of leaders.

You'll also learn about one of the sneakiest traps: the belief that 'leadership is just leadership'. It's sneaky because it seems so obviously true, but it's not. If you buy into this simplistic idea of leadership, then you will not pay enough attention to important new practices that are essential to your success as a leader of leaders.

The first step is to see and understand the traps and risks in believing that 'leadership is just leadership'.

The second step is to get clear on the opportunities that will open for you when you change your perspectives and practices. These changes will take you from being a successful professional contributor or leader of individuals to being a brilliant leader of leaders.

Your new role is a totally different job. It will take focus and effort to leave behind practices that served you well and to learn and adopt new practices. An important part of this is to realise that transitioning roles can be confusing and even overwhelming at times. But you'll also see that these challenging times are a healthy part of the process. In Part One, you'll discover what changes you need to make as part of your growth towards becoming a successful leader of leaders.

1

Letting go of what used to work

IT'S 7:30 ON A FRIDAY EVENING AND LISA IS STILL IN THE OFFICE, hunched over her laptop. She is vaguely aware of the whirr of the cleaner's vacuum, the darkness descending outside, and the glowing lights of the surrounding city. The last person to leave, one of her team leaders, headed out about two hours ago. They smiled and wished Lisa a great weekend. Lisa felt like screaming at them, 'Hey, I'm still here doing half of your frigging job!' But she didn't. She smiled and waved as she returned the 'great weekend' wish. 'Must keep the team positive,' she sighed to herself, hitting the keyboard with a little more intensity.

Lisa was so excited to get the promotion to the manager job leading a team of more than forty people, including six team leaders. She knew it was a great opportunity and a big step up. But after a month of this she was stressed, exhausted and disillusioned. It turned out to be like having forty children. All those open mouths coming at you all day with problems, with questions, with work they couldn't get done before 5pm, on top of all their petty fights and slights. And all of this for Lisa to sort out.

She gave it all she had. She had tried everything she knew to support her team. She listened patiently as people prattled on. She checked in regularly with as many people as she could, as often as she could. She answered people's questions and tried to resolve their disputes.

But tonight, as she sent off yet another text to her partner saying she would have to skip their dinner out, something in her seemed to snap. Lisa felt a rising wave of anger, frustration and exhaustion. She had tried it all, and it didn't seem to make the situation any better. She was so exhausted the numbers on the spreadsheet in front of her started dancing around. She slumped back in her chair and rubbed her eyes. For a moment, she left her hands covering her eyes. Darkness, quiet, peace.

'I can't go on like this!' she yelled at the empty office. The cleaner glanced up and then went back to his vacuuming. Lisa felt a kind of numbness, an emptiness inside. Slowly she packed up her things, loading her laptop into her bag. She walked over to the door, looked back, and turned out the light. For a moment she paused. This empty – totally empty – feeling.

In that moment, Lisa realised she was no longer stressed. She had given up. The lift arrived, and she walked in and pressed 'G'. 'Something's gotta give,' she said to her reflection in the lift mirror as she was whisked down to the empty city streets below.

What have I done?

Lisa had worked hard to get on top of her new role as a leader of leaders. As do many people in her position – perhaps including you! – Lisa had thought that she knew how to lead a team. She had been very successful in leading her previous team of five finance professionals, which was a major reason why she got the manager's job. Lisa had a reputation for being smart, dedicated and hardworking. She knew how the business worked inside and out, far more even than many of the senior leaders. She was highly respected as the go-to person for the tough questions and for her ability to translate the complexity of the business into clear directions and answers. But now she felt like she'd been thrown in the deep end and was sinking fast.

Do you feel the same?

After a few years working as a professional contributor in your field of expertise, you were so good at it that they made you the team leader. You may have even held a manager title. Perhaps you were a specialist in a very complex field such as finance, legal, actuarial or engineering – one in which it normally takes ten to fifteen years to become a team leader. And now the step into a more senior leadership role has happened, and you have multiple teams reporting to you. You are now a leader of leaders.

> *You knew it was going to be a stretch. You knew there would be a lot more to learn and a lot more responsibility. But you didn't think it would feel as out of control as this.*

You often hear yourself muttering 'Oh' as you discover something else you didn't know, face another expectation you weren't aware of, or get another invite to a regular meeting you didn't know you had to attend. In fact, your new experience can be summed up in three words:

- Overworked,
- Overwhelmed, and
- Over it.

Let's explore each.

Overworked

You are working much harder and much longer hours than you anticipated. The supposed "work hours" are chock-a-block with back-to-back meetings. Some days you struggle to find a few minutes to go to the bathroom! You end up doing the work that comes out of the meetings at night and on the weekend. Your usually neat 'to-do' list has taken on a life of its own, with more stuff being added each day than gets crossed off – if you even get the time to cross it off.

Overwhelmed

You are probably feeling a constant and increasing sense of overwhelm. It reminds you of that time as a kid when you were swimming at the beach and found yourself out past the breaking waves – out of your depth. How scarily accurate is that?

Yes, part of it is the volume of work, but it's more than that. There just seem to be so many people that you must relate to, so much more vital information to remember, and so many different kinds of information. And some of it really isn't information: it's more about subtle ideas, nuances, preferences, remembering what fits with what, and what decisions have what implications with everything else. You're smiling professionally on the surface, while underneath you're kicking like mad and trying to get a foothold on something solid.

Over it

And then there are the thoughts that start to drift through your mind – thoughts that surprise you and even disturb you. Thoughts like, 'I can't keep this up,' or 'This just isn't worth it,' or 'I'm over this, I'll just hang in long enough so it doesn't look too bad on my resume.'

These thoughts are disturbing because you knew this change would be big, but you didn't realise how different it would be. To hear yourself considering quitting really throws you off. Not

17

only that, but a kind of downward spiral cuts in as this mood starts to permeate every moment and seriously constricts your ability to do the job. You may even be asking yourself, 'What have I done?'

Something must give

Floundering around in the deep end can't go on forever. Something's gotta give. And something *will* give. It just depends on what you decide you want it to be.

There is an increasing body of research that points to the negative impact of long working hours and workplace stress on both the health of individuals and the performance of the organisation. Research published in the *American Heart Association Journal* found that, out of more than 143,000 participants, those who worked ten or more hours a day for at least fifty days per year had a 29% greater risk of stroke.[1]

Your health can 'give'

The first things to go when you are floundering in the deep end include rest and sleep, time for exercise, and good eating habits. You slip into a glass of something at the end of the day to help you wind down. Then you need a couple of cups of coffee in

---

1 https://newsroom.heart.org/news/
long-work-hours-associated-with-increased-risk-of-stroke?preview=a9a5

the morning to counter the effect of the glasses from the night before and the lack of sleep that inevitably flows from that. The extra coffee and the heightened, alert physiology of your day will then require some more glasses to help you wind down at the end of the day.

And so the cycle rolls on. Over time, your physical and mental health will erode. You'll put on a little weight. The anxiety state will continue longer.

> You'll start to run out of energy, and the constant state of tiredness will become a weariness that will slide into despair.

The results can 'give'

You may be able to hold things together enough to get the short-term stuff over the line. But over the medium term, say six to twelve months, the results of your teams will start to slip, and then decline. This will further fuel your growing anxiety. Depending on the organisation you're working in, your bosses may cut you some slack. But you'll only be able to play the 'I'm new' card for so long.

Your career can 'give'

This one probably won't happen in the short term, but if the decline of your health and the slip of results continues without you doing something to change it, it's only a matter of time before you fail in your new role. Failure in your first major leadership role is not necessarily fatal for your career – unless you don't change anything in your approach. If you end up blaming the organisation, your boss or your team, then your own perspective will have pushed your career to the edge of the cliff.

Other areas of your life can 'give'

I bet you have already experienced the earlier stages of this one. The anxiety, exhaustion and moodiness of grinding remorselessness will start to seep into every aspect of your life. You start to pull out of social times with family and friends because you have work to do. You can't do the weekend away because you have stuff to get ready for the next week. Even when you can get your body to physically be home or at the café or the park, you aren't really there. You find yourself only half-listening. You feel your face smiling in contrast with your actual mood of despair. Relationships grow shallow, and then distant.

Working harder won't work

To try to compensate for all this, you are likely to do what many dedicated professionals do: you work even harder and crank up the work hours even more.

But the reason you are floundering is because you are working harder and harder using the practices that made you successful in your previous role, not this one.

Things will not get better through working harder.

Although your current experience might not feel that great, one upside of your present situation is that you're realising you must change if you are going to survive and grow as a leader of leaders. It's important to really listen and pay attention to what you are experiencing right now. Move forward into the chaos and pain. This may seem like strange advice, but disruptive experiences like this will expose your old learnings and assumptions, if you are open to observing what is going on. The way forward is not in hoping that something will change in the world around you, but in seeing what must change *in you*.

Breaking the cycle

You are entering one of the most significant transitions in your career. The demands have increased significantly. The stakes are high. So, how can you start to break out of the cycle of burning more hours and energy for less impact and results? Here are some important starting points.

Stay in the pain

It's natural to recoil from pain – and that goes for emotional pain as well as physical pain. No one enjoys feeling anxious, stressed, out of control and out of their depth. Us humans are experts at avoiding pain. We'll try pretty much anything to stop it – especially by denying that we have a problem at all, and instead blaming other people or our circumstances.

With this transition, it's important that you stay in the pain – that you face the reality of what you are experiencing by allowing yourself to feel the pain and discomfort without fighting against it and without assessing it as a deficiency in yourself. This pain can serve you by giving you the energy to change and opening you up to where you need to change.

Be open, not constricted

As you experience the growth pains of this transition, you will likely be constricting yourself. Your eyes narrow, your jaw tightens, and your body draws into itself. Your body, your mind and your emotions constrict, and your options and possibilities seem to narrow.

What is important in this transition is to open up to new experiences, new ways of seeing things, and new ways of getting things done. You can start by opening your body by relaxing your eyes, your jaw or neck, and the muscles of the rest of your body. This will help you to loosen up and open your current interpretations and assessments to change.

Listen to yourself

This opening up will help you to start listening to yourself. Listening to yourself includes listening to what you are feeling, what you are thinking, and how you are interpreting your experience. Being able to do this is essential for change and growth. It's through this that you can start to do the work of unlearning old ways and learning new ones.

Delete the belief that 'leadership is the same everywhere'

There are two common beliefs that you must delete. The first one is that leadership is a generic set of skills that are basically the same no matter the role and organisation you are in. You can see this approach in a lot of leadership books and courses, but the practices that make for a successful leader can vary a lot from organisation to organisation and role to role. This is especially true for becoming a leader of leaders. Accepting the idea that 'leadership is the same everywhere' blinds you to the changes you must face and leaves you resting on the leadership practices from your past role, which might not apply so well to this one.

Delete the belief that 'what got you success before will get you success now'

The second common belief that you must delete is a more subtle assumption: the idea that what got you to where you are is what will continue to give you success.

In some ways, it's very natural to keep doing the things that have been working for you. Yes, some of the knowledge, skills and practices that you have from your first team-leader role will still be useful as a leader of leaders, but not all of them. Some of them you will keep, and some you will need to leave behind. The important thing is that you become aware of the unquestioned beliefs you have about success.

For example, I know a senior leader in a large healthcare organisation who was a star that people loved as an individual contributor, and then as a leader of small clinical teams. His teams loved him because they felt they were supported when he regularly, closely checked their technical work. They loved the sense of clarity they got from how he specified work processes in great detail.

Now, a senior leader, this person takes exactly the same approach but with very negative effects. The leaders who report to him feel stifled and micromanaged. Much of the best talent has left, and his organisation struggles to recruit leaders because his reputation is now widespread.

The bottom line is that some of the things that are important to succeeding as a team leader can get in the way of becoming a successful leader of leaders.

> *When we are thrown in the deep end, we always sink first. But by staying with the pain, opening and listening to yourself, you will find your way to the surface.*

Your experience is normal

You are not weird or inadequate – you are a human like everyone else around you. Your experience of this transition, growth and change is normal. That's right: normal and natural.

Your confusion and sense of feeling lost is a sign that your old ways-of-being and -acting are breaking down. This is an essential phase in making the change. Perspectives and assumptions that you were blind to before are now clear and obvious to you. This means you can do something about them.

If your experience is normal and is a sign of old ways breaking, then you have reason to hope that you are on the way to becoming a leader of leaders. For some reason we don't often use the word 'hope' in our working lives, but hope is essential to any human effort – especially to change and growth.

You'll start to understand what perspectives and practices are getting in the way of you growing into your new role. This can only happen as you open up and as you listen to yourself. This is how you will gain insights into how you are trying to do things now.

This listening is also how you will discover new perspectives and practices that will enable you to make the transition to being a leader of leaders. Some of the new ways are very different from your old ways.

> *Some or even a lot of these practices will feel strange and uncomfortable as you first try them out.*

Leaders in transition

Recent research conducted by Dr Ty Wiggins from the University of Wollongong found that leadership transitions can be the most stressful and challenging experiences in a person's career and life. Dr Wiggins' in-depth interviews with a wide range of leaders highlighted that many people making leadership transitions are thrown in the deep end.

His research also discovered that:

- Leadership transitions, including those associated with being promoted, are happening more frequently due to the increasing pace of business change. As organisations are changing faster and more often, the chance of finding yourself transitioning to a leader-of-leaders role is increasing. And this change may happen with very little warning.

- The positive reputation you have from your previous role or previous organisation is a great help at first, but you can't bank on it to get you through this change. Human memory is short, and fame is fleeting. Your great success on an important project will pass into history, and the people that loved you as a leader also move on.

- Arriving in the role with enthusiasm and energy is always important. People are always more drawn to a motivated leader than a bland, demotivated one. But unless your enthusiasm is quickly matched by impact and results, it wears thin after a while.

- Failure to make the transition costs the organisation and team a lot, but the person themselves can also experience damage to their career and confidence. Leadership is deeply personal work. When your professional confidence takes a hit, it can go very deep and take a lot of time and work to recover from.

- Often there is a lack of support for leaders making this transition. This can occur both if you take a more senior leadership role in another organisation, or in your existing organisation.

- The factors that drive transition success are more associated with the individual's mindset and practices than the support of the organisation.

So although you may feel like you are sinking now, there is a lot you can do to drive your own success.

IDEAS FOR ACTION

1. Start listening to and capturing your thoughts and feelings. Keep a journal of what you are going through. This will start to reveal your old learnings and assumptions and point you to specific areas that need change.

2. Start to listen for the old beliefs that 'leadership is just leadership' and 'what got me success before will get me success now'.

3. Remind yourself every day that you are a learner. A learner mindset is a significant driver of success through times of change and uncertainty.

4. Watch your health and well-being. Don't go all hard on yourself, but pay attention to your mental and physical health.

5. Book fifteen minutes at the end of each week to stop, reflect on, and write down what you have learned that week.

QUESTIONS TO DIG DEEPER

1. How are you really feeling right now? What are the specific emotions that you are experiencing?

2. How long can you really sustain the pace and intensity at which you are working? One month? Three months? Six months? The end of the week?

3. How is all this affecting your health and life as a whole? Who might it be important to share all this with?

UP NEXT

In this chapter we explored how becoming a leader of leaders is a transition to a totally different job. We looked at the experience you may be having as you try to do this new role using the assumptions and practices from your previous role. We also looked at how important it is to make this change for yourself and the organisation.

In Chapter 2, we'll look at how different your new senior leadership role is, and what the experience of this important transition can be like. We'll also point out some of the derailers that can arise through the process, and introduce the pathway of change.

2

From overworked to influential

FIVE YEARS AGO, JONATHAN GOT A JOB AS THE MANAGER of a small team within a large government agency doing some interesting but narrow research using data collected from a variety of sources in the health, safety and well-being field. Little did he know how much his job would grow and how much his life would change.

Before taking this role, Jonathan had been an occupational therapist working in the state government's rehabilitation services. During his university studies, he had become interested in exploring broader trends in workplace accidents, rather than just looking at the specific needs of an individual. His position as manager of this small research team was an ideal role for him, as he could now spend his time exploring interesting research questions with like-minded professional and individual contributors. Although he was officially the team's manager, it didn't really feel like a management job: most of Jonathan's focus and energy was directed towards working with data to discover trends and insights.

Over the following five years, the team's work was noticed more and more for the important insights they were discovering. These insights started to be seen as invaluable for informing government policy and business practices. So, more and more organisations began to use the team's research to help them understand important policy issues. All this coincided with advances in technology and data analytics, which created even more demand for the team's services.

About four years into this growth, the team had increased from five to over forty people. By then, Jonathan was very stressed and exhausted from working until late almost every night of the week in order to stay on top of the workload, and often large chunks of the weekend as well. This increasing strain had led Jonathan to yell at some people on his team a couple of times – which was not at all like the Jonathan that his team members knew. He was growing frustrated with the team, and especially with his direct reports, because they kept coming around with the same questions all the time. Also, there were constant arguments among the team members over who was supposed to do what. The blame game was endless, and eventually the turnaround times on projects started to blow out, which caused customer satisfaction measures to drop.

Jonathan was working hard to keep it all going. He knew he probably needed to change a lot of things, but he never had the time or energy to do anything about it. He told himself that he had to make all the decisions, because if he didn't then people would make the wrong decisions. Jonathan was constantly sorting out conflicts between team members at *all* levels.

> *Nothing that used to work seemed to work anymore.*

What Jonathan eventually came to realise was that he was now in a completely different job from the one he had started four years earlier. He loved the work the team did, but he could also see clearly now that the job he and the team did had led to their workload going through the roof. They were victims of their own success.

Different pathways to results

Jonathan's job changed gradually, but radically. This was tricky, because gradual shifts in your role are not as obvious compared to moving into a totally new role. Rather, Jonathan was stuck in a situation that many people in his position find themselves in: the mindsets and practices that generate your success become deeply embedded, and you get caught in the trap of thinking that what worked in the past will work in the future. If you have led a team, you can lead another team, you tell yourself. People are people, after all.

But while some of the skills from your team-leader role will be helpful in future roles, the leader-of-leaders role must be thought of as a completely new and different job. Figure 1 below shows why.

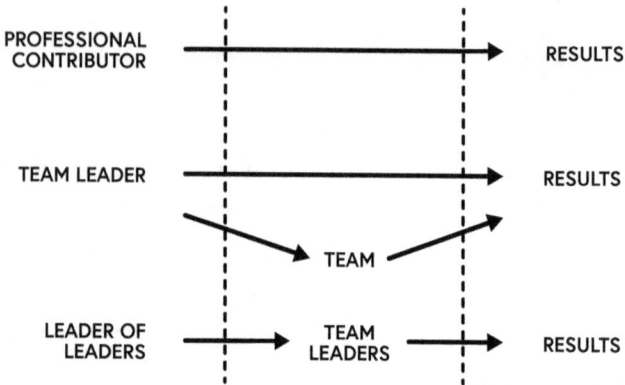

Figure 1. Getting results in three management levels

The figure above shows the transition from professional contributor and team leader to leader of leaders. It also illustrates the flow that each role must follow in order to achieve results.

Let's take a closer look at each of these roles and the differences between them. Each of these roles involves dealing with people, but in significantly different ways.

The transition from team leader to leader of leaders is a much bigger change than you anticipate.

	PROFESSIONAL CONTRIBUTOR	TEAM LEADER	LEADER OF LEADERS
Role	To apply your professional knowledge and skills to produce products/services	To coordinate the workflow of your team to ensure technical proficiency	To design and shape the work system to ensure sustained and continually adapting products/services
Practices	• Define technical problems and opportunities • Apply knowledge to solve problems or organise processes • Fix or refine technical products/services to ensure they meet requirements	• Be knowledgeable about the work of your team (in most cases you are still doing some of the work as well as being the leader of the team) • Closely monitor and coordinate the workflow of the team • Quickly solve operational and technical problems as they come up • Make sure the team follows procedures and practices	• Scan the environment for emerging trends and changes • Sustain connections to the wider internal and external work system • Collaborate with other leaders to ensure the work systems continue to deliver relevant products/services • Provide structure and space for team leaders to lead
Results	Individual products/services	Products/services produced by team members and the individual	Products/services as outcomes of integrated teams and systems

Table 1. Roles and responsibilities of individuals at different management levels

A time for change

Making the transition to each of these very different roles doesn't happen overnight. Yes, you can change your title, change your workspace, and even change the people you work with, but that doesn't actually mean you have changed your job.

I don't want to kid you or give you a light answer that will make you feel good but won't work in the real world. The fact is, it takes significant personal growth and change to adapt to each of these different jobs, and especially so when you become a leader of leaders.

There is a wonderful capability that we human beings have to learn something so deeply and so thoroughly that we get to the point where we can do things without really thinking about it. (Psychologists call this 'internalising'.) The best example of this is driving a car. Once you have been driving a car for over two years, you can drive to places you go to regularly without conscious thought about steering, braking, gear-changing, or what street to turn into. Like cleaning our teeth in the morning, we can do all this on automatic pilot.

The same principle applies to the job you did previously. If you were a successful team leader, you could perform all of the responsibilities of that role without even having to think about them. This is what it feels like when we reach full competence in a job.

The consequences of not realising that the leader-of-leaders role is a totally different job are devastating for the individual leader, as well as costly and inefficient for the organisation they work in.

The risks of derailing are high

These consequences are most often gradual. They sneak up on you, and they take time to flood out into the organisation around you. Most of the changes that are important to make this transition successfully are nuanced and initially unseen.

Let's look at the risks of not actively making this transition as soon as you can.

For you, the new leader of leaders:

- Feelings of stress and burnout

- Negative impacts on relationships outside of work

- Loss of touch with reality and exclusion from important conversations

- Disconnection from your peers, your direct-report leaders and other team members

- Focusing on the wrong details to maintain a facade of control

- Mental or physical illness

For the team and the organisation:

- Inefficiency creeps in when the new leader disempowers team leaders to make improvements and work with peers to solve whole-system problems

- Good team leaders get sick of the micromanagement and leave

- Team performance drops away as the team's efforts fragment due to a lack of integration with the organisation at a broad level

- The lack of integration and engagement seeps into the customer experience, with customers being shunted between teams and no team member taking ownership of solving customer problems

If enough of these consequences actually happen, it can lead to the derailment of your career. The word 'derailing' really captures this idea. What might start as a kink in the track or a rock on the rails can quickly throw everything off. Your reputation may decline, support and goodwill from your peers may drift away, or you may end up dismissed or marginalised and avoided by people around you.

The good news is that the person who has the biggest influence on these transitions is you. You can shift your perspective and your actions to stop this derailing from happening. Once you understand how deep the need for a new approach is, you are ready to make the change.

Making the change

Making the change to become an effective leader of leaders can be a demanding stretch. While it's never a neat step-by-step process, there are some distinct phases and experiences that people typically go through, and knowing this general framework can help you navigate the transition experience. You'll most likely bounce around between the phases, but the lower phases are all part of the journey. They are important indicators that the way you are used to doing things is no longer working. This breakdown is what will open you up to moving into different ways of working.

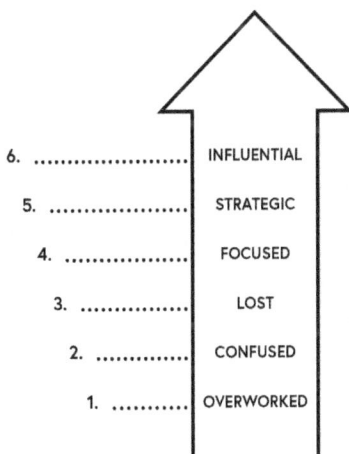

6. .... INFLUENTIAL

5. .... STRATEGIC

4. .... FOCUSED

3. .... LOST

2. .... CONFUSED

1. .... OVERWORKED

Figure 2. From overworked to influential

1. Overworked

We often try to do our new leader-of-leaders role by relying on the way-of-being and practices that worked for us in the past – especially if we enjoyed some success in these previous roles. One of the first signs that this approach is not working in our new role is that we end up working harder and longer without coming any closer to 'getting on top of' the new role. Even the idea of 'getting on top of the new role' is itself a hangover from simpler roles that had a more fixed shape and parameters. We do what used to work, and we push it until we reach a point like Lisa did: we end up exhausted and frustrated.

> *As difficult as this phase can be, reaching this point is the first step towards becoming a true leader of leaders.*

2. Confused

The moment of realising that doing what you used to do isn't working is often followed by a period of confusion. You know what you have been doing isn't working, so you try to grab onto something – anything – as long as it's different from what you are doing now. You may look for a quick fix or a simple technique that you think might make the difference, but you still find yourself drifting back to the practices that you know, because the days keep coming and you must try *something*.

This isn't an enjoyable experience, but what is happening is that the pain is waking us up. In our day-to-day working life, a crack has appeared in our familiar approaches, reactions and responses. This crack is the start of an opening through which we begin to observe ourselves.

> We start to come off automatic pilot and start to look at what we are feeling, what we are thinking, the language we are using to make sense of these new experiences, and what the impact of these things is on ourselves and the world around us.

3. Lost

The confusion described above is about struggle. It's about wrestling with the job. It can sometimes lead you to drift into blaming other people for your experience: 'If only my direct-report leaders were better,' 'If only my boss would be more supportive,' 'The culture of this team is so bad' … the list goes on.

But then you reach the point where you feel like you don't have the energy to struggle anymore. All the other techniques and tweaks you tried didn't really change things either. In a sense, you give up. And sometimes, people *really* give up: they quit.

Now, there's nothing wrong with quitting. You should always have the key to that escape hatch in your back pocket. Depending on the specifics of yourself and your situation, that may be the way to go. But this feeling of being lost is also an essential and healthy place to get to on your path to becoming a leader of leaders.

Think about it for a moment. You tried pushing your old ways harder and harder, and ended up overworked. You tried to grab onto anything else you could, and ended up confused. Now you have arrived at this feeling of being lost. It might not feel this way, but believe me – this is progress!

You have given up on what you know, and stopped relying on the past. You are now ready and open to move into the new, different and unfamiliar. Sometimes we must get to this place of feeling lost to move on. This phase can also be experienced as a kind of 'breakdown': it's as if the old vehicle has broken down and we don't know what to do next. The writer Rafael Echeverria referred to this experience as sitting in the 'Space of Nothingness'.

> *Your old ways are gone, but the new way is yet to emerge.*

4. Focused

The result of the 'lost' phase is that you now have a clean, blank sheet of paper. The previous phases are like a clearing-out of your assumptions and prior learnings, which now presents you with an opportunity to focus. To take advantage of this opportunity, you must ask yourself these three questions:

- What is this role about?

- What is the unique value of this role?

- What are the most important things to do now?

By answering these questions, you start to move into the next phase of your growth as a leader of leaders – you start to focus. And this is not only a vital phase in your transition, but also something you will need to do every single day as you continue in your new role. The scope and span of most leader-of-leader roles means that there will always be more to do and more that could possibly be done. There will be endless opportunities for improvement, change, new technologies, new operating models, new everything. Focus is an essential everyday practice for leaders of leaders.

It's in this phase that your openness, curiosity and just plain desperation will lead you to seek out help. This help can take many forms: for example, it could be a person, a book, a blog, a podcast, or a mentor or coach. If we put this stage in terms of the model presented in Figure 1, you're now at the moment when you've decided to become a leader of leaders, instead of remaining a team leader or a professional contributor.

Gradually, some clarity of purpose starts to emerge from the confusion.

5. Strategic

In this phase, rather than leaping around trying different techniques to fix the situation, your new focus will enable you to start constructing your area of responsibility, your team, and the system they work in.

The unique role that you have in this phase is to build the scope and span of your team leaders. This is the most significant shift from being a team leader. For most people coming into their first leader-of-leaders role, this is where you will learn a lot and where you will do things differently. The big shift is in creating enough spaces for your team leaders to truly lead.

Whether the role you are moving into is newly created or well-established will determine how much of this work has already been done. I call this 'shaping the sandbox'. A sandbox is a space with clear boundaries in which people can make decisions and take action. You don't have to lock yourself away and work all this out on your own – in fact, the work context is usually too complex for you to be able to do that even if you wanted to. Instead, you can call on your reporting leaders to work with you on this, as they will have important insights and knowledge that you don't have. And, of course, the more they have a say in the shaping of the sandbox, the more engaged they will be in making it work as well.

The world changes constantly, and so constructing sandboxes is not a one-off challenge but an open and ongoing project for you and your direct-report leaders. Is the sandbox the best it can be to achieve great results?

6. Influential

Now that you have clarified your focus and the unique value of your role and have started to actively shape your area of responsibility, you are ready to act on the next phase of becoming a leader of leaders – influencing to integrate.

An essential dimension of the role of leader of leaders is to make sure that the work and outcomes of your team are integrated with the efforts of the rest of your organisation, and with the experiences of the customers who get value from the outcomes your team produce. You start to look at your teams and their work in the broader context of your organisation and other teams, especially your peer leaders. This is an important step that many leaders of leaders don't pay enough attention to.

Influencing to integrate is about building constructive working relationships with other senior leaders so that the work of your teams connects with that of other teams to build a seamless, effective total organisation. New leaders of leaders sometimes write off influencing to integrate as just playing politics, but these two concepts are fundamentally different. If you are taking action to build a more effective organisation – even if that process entails arguments, conversation and conflict – then you are by definition influencing to integrate. If, on the other hand, you are taking action to push your own personal interests and agenda, you are playing politics. Playing politics reduces integration and creates more inefficiencies as people burn time and energy protecting their own turf.

Your goal is always to improve the effectiveness and performance of the whole organisation, not big-note yourself or try to bring someone else down.

Expanding your possibilities

Your ability to successfully lead other leaders is the core capability you need to do bigger and more senior leadership roles. It's this ability that enables you to lead larger and larger sections of organisations, and even whole organisations. Your first essential step in building this capability is letting go of many of the mindsets and practices that have worked well for you so far.

This will feel strange and even scary at first. That's why going through the transition steps from 'overworked' to 'influential' is vital. Don't back away from the change. Use the model in Figure 2 as a map to guide you and help you make sense of what you are going through.

If you develop the mindsets and practices covered in the rest of this book, you will be able to open up your career prospects to more senior leadership roles. And, of course, this can also expand your financial possibilities as well.

> *Once you are successful in your first transition to a leader of leaders, you can do it again and again.*

Individual genius to leader of leaders

Cara was a genius professional contributor working in a large media company. She really was a genius, with a strong reputation in her organisation and in the wider market by the time she was in her mid-twenties.

She was now moving into a new leadership role, which was a significant step up to a leader-of-leaders role. She had six direct-report leaders under her, and a total team of around sixty people across a diverse range of skills and occupations. As a result, Cara was overworked when she first moved into her new role. Her days were spent reacting and 'putting out spot fires'. She worked late every day and a lot of her weekend, but she just didn't seem to be 'getting on top of things'. She was feeling totally overwhelmed, and was really annoyed by anyone who got in the way of her getting her work done. Everything felt out of control.

At this point, Cara was already in the 'confused' phase of her journey, and had begun drifting into the 'lost' phase. Fortunately, she was very open to new ways of working and new leadership practices. Her first big breakthrough was grasping the unique value of her role as the shaper of the team through her team leaders. This insight led her into a series of important actions that transformed her approach to her role. She introduced more one-on-one collaboration with her direct-report leaders. She started putting emphasis on people, culture, and the individual growth of her team members. She started taking a more whole-system approach to problems and opportunities and moved more into the role of painting the big picture for the team, exposing them to the broader context in which they were doing their work, and continually reminding them of the important purpose they were living and delivering.

As a result, Cara got her life back and began to experience new levels of job satisfaction by seeing the broader impact she could have as a leader of leaders.

IDEAS FOR ACTION

1. Even if you are not yet in a leader-of-leaders role, be alert to gradual changes in your leadership role, especially as team leaders, even of small teams, start reporting to you.

2. Use the model in Figure 1 to assess and monitor the changes in your role.

3. Review the experiences you've had in your role and examine them for early signs of emerging derailers.

4. Write a list of what you would like to achieve in your new leader-of-leaders role.

5. Use your imagination to write a news report describing you and your experiences as you master your new leadership role. You can use this to visualise your success and start to shift your mindset. By imagining your success, you start to prime yourself to do what it takes to succeed. This will also help to build your enthusiasm about this new and different phase of your life.

QUESTIONS TO DIG DEEPER

1. After reading this chapter, what excites you about the possibilities of being a leader of leaders?

2. What are you most concerned about in making the transition to senior leadership? Why?

3. Looking further into the future, what possibilities can you imagine for your career when you make the change to senior leadership?

UP NEXT

In this chapter we looked at three different roles – professional contributor, team leader, and leader of leaders – and how each of them achieves results. We saw how transitioning into a new role will be a time of significant change for you. There are some risks, and there are also great possibilities. We also explored what the experience of this change is like.

Part Two of this book tells you how to go about becoming a successful leader of leaders. In Chapter 3 we'll explore the first driver of this change – your way-of-being. We'll look at what your way-of-being is, and how you can adapt it as an important step in making the transition.

PART TWO:

MAKING THE CHANGE

Now that you know why you need to step up and adapt to your new role, you can start to make the changes required to do just that. In Part Two, you'll discover the four important domains of growth to become a leader of leaders, which are shown in Figure 3 below. You can work on many of them at the same time, but as you can see in the model, adapting your way-of-being and giving yourself a promotion are at the core of your growth. The upcoming chapters will give you a deeper understanding of what to do in each of these domains of growth.

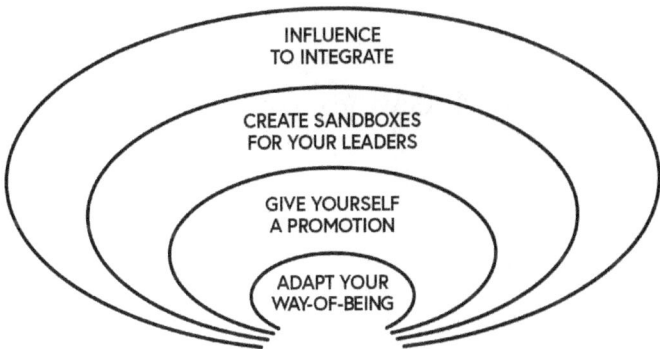

Figure 3. The four domains of growth to becoming a leader of leaders

Chapter 3: Adapt your way-of-being

Your way-of-being is how you experience and make sense of the world around you. It plays a crucial role in senior leadership positions, where so much of what you do is about working out what's going on and what must happen to achieve what's important. How you experience your workday moment to moment is the result of a dynamic, constant interplay between three dimensions:

- the language you use;

- your emotions and moods; and

- the way you hold yourself physically.

This 'way-of-being' model will give you easy-to-use practices to become a better observer of your own temperament at any moment. The ability to constantly observe your way-of-being and how you are presenting yourself to the world is at the core of becoming a leader of leaders.

Chapter 4: Give yourself a promotion

We get used to thinking about ourselves in a particular role; we even use our roles to define ourselves when we first meet people (for example, 'I'm the manager of…' or 'I'm a business analyst'). The label we give ourselves shapes how we think, and what we think influences what we say and do. This is why the next phase in becoming a leader of leaders is to promote yourself in your own head: to consciously and actively use the language of your new role to unlearn old habits and become open to learning new ones.

Chapter 5: Create sandboxes for your leaders

Now you can start to turn your attention to the next circle, which is the leaders who report to you. Creating sandboxes for your leaders is all about the space you give them to play. It's about giving them the freedom and support to make real decisions over resources and work processes, so that they really can be leaders to their own teams. In Chapter 5, you'll learn an easy-to-remember model and process for creating and sustaining sandboxes that give your leaders space to learn and grow.

Chapter 6: Influence to integrate

As a leader of leaders, an important and often neglected part of your job is to make sure the work of your teams remains relevant and valuable in an environment in which nothing stays still and everything is in a constant state of change. In this phase, you'll learn the practices that will help you keep a lively flow between you, your team, and the wider world. Being able to coordinate the operational flow of many teams is the highest value of your role, and is often a new area of work for people becoming leaders of leaders.

> *By doing the work in each of the phases, you'll make the transition from overworked and confused to being a leader of leaders.*

3

Adapt your way-of-being

WHEN I FIRST MET MEGAN, SHE TALKED FAST, AND A LOT. SHE had two mobile phones that she checked constantly. Her new boss was driving her crazy. Megan felt she had to stay on her boss's case all the time to keep them on track. Although she was experienced in similar senior roles as an executive officer to senior leaders and a senior troubleshooter, Megan was now in her first leader-of-leaders role, and had four direct-report leaders with small, highly specialised teams.Megan cared a lot about her work, and genuinely wanted to do what was best for the organisation and the people it served. But while she didn't realise it at first, she was getting in her own way.

Her background as a fixer and troubleshooter meant that her default settings were about fixing immediate problems by telling people what they should do. She did this bluntly, and without fear or favour. In the past, this approach had really worked for her: Megan had held some amazing roles and fixed some big problems. But in her new leader-of-leaders role, she was floundering. She was stressed, frustrated, felt unsupported, hated her job, and felt like she was just bouncing off her boss all the time. If it weren't for her big mortgage, she would have quit.

Megan was looking for techniques to 'make' her boss be different. Gradually, she shifted her focus to what was going on for her in this experience. Megan became aware of how her focus was on the way her boss was acting. She started to realise the link between the language she was using in her own head about the situation she was in, how this shaped her mood, and how she held herself in meetings with her boss. Specifically, she started to notice that when her boss didn't immediately answer, Megan would run a story in her head about how her boss was excluding her from what was really going on.

The breakthrough for Megan was to see and feel how these interpretations triggered bodily responses in her that generated a mood of resentment. Thoughts like, 'I am hard done by, and I will get revenge' swirled in her head. This would then lead to a mood of resignation, with thoughts like, 'There is no hope of this changing, so I might as well give up.' Together, all of this indicated that Megan was suffering from performance anxiety, overwork and confusion. She realised that she wasn't interpreting the world the right way.

Armed with this insight, Megan started to make changes in her interpretations, her mood, and how she physically held herself.

As she did, she noticed that meetings with her boss started to change. They became calmer and slower, and her boss started to open up more about what she was thinking and what was going on in the larger context.

> *Megan came to the powerful insight that it was she herself who had become calmer and slower, and that realization created an important shift in her relationship with her boss.*

All this meant that Megan was now getting important, broader information from her boss that she could use to shape the priorities, organisation and work of her team.

Your way-of-being

To succeed in her new role, Megan realised she had to adapt. Not adapt in some big, global way, but quickly and in the moment. Leadership opportunities happen in moments: moments of sense-making, moments of relationship-building, and moments of decision-making. In an ever-changing and unpredictable world, a leader's ability to adapt in the moment can make the difference between responding quickly and effectively to your environment or getting stuck in old ways that no longer deliver results.

In the nitty-gritty of your day, what does it mean to adapt? How do you do it? This is where the idea of your way-of-being is very powerful and practical.

Your way-of-being is the overall state you are in at any moment of the day. It is how you are or feel most of the time.

What comes to mind when you stop and consciously think about how you are? What you might become aware of is things like the mood you are in, what you have been thinking about recently, and what you are experiencing physically, such as whether you are tense or relaxed. In our moment-to-moment existence, all these dimensions come together in one whole and integrated experience. The model of your way-of-being illustrated in Figure 4 below was developed by Rafael Echeverria and Julio Olalla and described in Alan Sieler's series of books *Coaching to the Human Soul*.

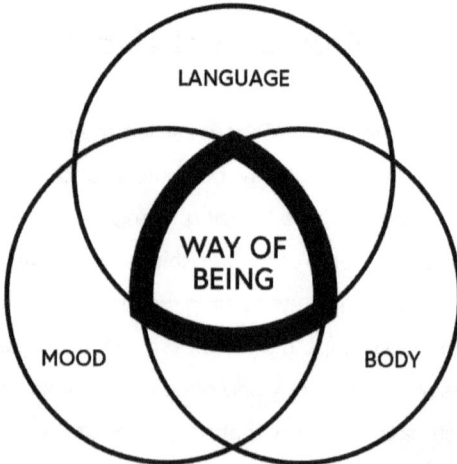

Figure 4. Way-of-being

You can see that our way-of-being in the world at any moment in time is the result of biologically driven interactions between the *language* we are using to make sense of our experience, our *body* (nervous system, physiology and body shape), and the emotions and *mood* we are in.

> *The key point is that this interaction is dynamic.*
> *Each of the elements triggers the others and*
> *then feeds back into the whole system.*

The concept of way-of-being was developed from the work of researchers who were exploring the biology of cognition, a discipline that studies how we perceive and process our experience in the world through a biological perspective, rather than the more common psychological perspective. (The philosophy of Martin Heidegger, as detailed in his famous book *Being and Time* – which actually uses the expression 'way-of-being' – was also a powerful influence in the popularization of this concept.) The pioneers of this area of study were two biologists from Chile, Humberto Maturana and Francisco Varela, whose analysis of the workings of animal eyes led them to discover that humans' experience of the world is determined by the state of our nervous system.

The practical application of Maturana and Varela's research, which has been developed by such writers as Alan Sieler in his four-volume series *Coaching to the Human Soul*, comes from this fundamental insight: our experience, perception and interpretation of the world are physically and physiologically driven.

Why not learning?

Working on shifting our way-of-being is a similar idea to the concept of 'learning'. 'Learning' is likely to be a more familiar term for you than 'way-of-being', but 'learning' often has a rather narrow meaning in the world of business and organisations.

Often, 'learning' is thought of as simply taking in information. But we all know the difference between knowing *about* something and truly *learning* something. I can take in all the information in the world about how to ride a bike, and that may be interesting and helpful as I imagine myself riding a bike for the first time; I might even tell my friend that I have learned how to ride a bike by reading the *Encyclopedia of Bicycles*. But having this information doesn't mean I can actually *ride* a bike. Possessing information and applying it to real life are two different things.

I will really start *learning* about how to ride a bike when I actually get on it and start trying to ride (and no doubt fall off). Bits of information I have in my head from the *Encyclopedia of Bicycles* may come to mind as I wobble down the street, and they might help me. But real learning only happens when I engage in the activity with my whole being – the language I am using to make sense of the experience, the movement and shaping of my body, and the mood I am in as I try, fail, and try again. The experience of mastering bike-riding involves our whole way-of-being. Becoming a leader of leaders is the same.

The idea of our way-of-being captures the dynamic that goes on in us when we are truly learning.

Putting it into practice

To understand how our way-of-being works, let's look at one of the most common experiences that new leaders face: participating in meetings with senior leaders who they have previously not had much to do with. Most people experience some level of nervousness or anxiety when they first start attending new meetings. It goes to a whole new level when you must present to the group and participate in robust conversations.

These scenarios are clear examples of the influence your way-of-being has on your impact as a leader. Imagine you are required to present the business plan and budget for your area of responsibility. You will be presenting to the most senior leader in your organisation (the CEO, or perhaps the department secretary), the head of the finance team, three other senior leaders, and your boss. (Frankly, even as you start to *imagine* this scenario you may be experiencing some changes in your way-of-being!)

Let's say it's two hours before the meeting. You've got your presentation together, and you are sitting in a meeting room going through it. What might your way-of-being look like in that moment?

1. **Body –** you might be hunched over your laptop with your jaw and facial muscles tight as you strain and strive to remember your key points and imagine the questions that the head of finance will ask.

2. **Mood** – very anxious. You have been in previous meetings where the head of finance really carved up one of your peers.

3. **Language** – perhaps thoughts like these are going through your head: 'John really got carved up when he presented last week.' 'What if I can't answer a question the head of finance asks?' 'I can get a real brain-freeze when I'm put on the spot. Gee, I hope that doesn't happen today.' Sometimes there are even deeper narratives running through your head, like 'I feel like a total fraud!' or 'I actually have no idea what I'm talking about,' or 'I'm just a kid from the country – what am I doing here!'

As these three dimensions hum along, they dynamically influence each other. Your body responds to your self-talk by tightening, sending out some shots of adrenaline, and trying to make itself small to protect you from your fear of the wrath of the head of finance. You experience all this as a ramping-up of your anxiety. You can sense your brain starting to scramble and get distracted by all this stuff going on in your system.

You turn up at the meeting. The head of finance has her head down, studying her laptop screen, and doesn't respond to your somewhat shaky 'Good morning'. 'Just as I thought,' you say to yourself, 'She's going to carve me up.' Your body is tense now, so you fumble with your laptop and have trouble connecting to the room presentation system. You turn around and knock over someone's glass of water, which splatters all over the conference table. You feel like you want to cry. Before you know it, you are up at the front trying to talk through your presentation. You struggle to string words together, and your throat is dry. You hear yourself starting to apologise for how you are speaking and for not knowing the answers to some questions. Finally, your presentation is over, and you slump into your seat looking at the floor.

How effective do you think you would be in the meeting? What impact do you think your way-of-being might have on whether your plan and budget get accepted?

You can see that the language or narrative we run in our head triggers our body and physiology as it tries to prepare you for what you have told it is a major threat. The dynamic interplay between your language and your body generates your mood of anxiety. The experience of this mood of anxiety then triggers more negative self-talk to explain the physiological experience, which ramps the whole system up even further.

> *Our responses to the world around us and how we make sense of our experiences in the world is formed by the state of our nervous system and physiological well-being.*

So, what has all this got to do with being a leader of leaders? Everything. The important work of senior leaders happens in the moments of each day. If your interpretations, interactions and decisions as a leader are generated by your way-of-being in each moment, then your way-of-being is at the core of your effectiveness and impact as a leader.

Let's explore this a bit further.

Shaping your world

In the example above, we explored a very specific scenario in which your way-of-being had a clear and significant impact on your influence and impact as a leader. Your way-of-being also plays a more fundamental role in your transition to becoming a leader of leaders. We adopt different ways-of-being for the different roles we are in. When you moved into your first team-leader role, you developed a certain way-of-being that enabled you to be successful in that role.

In most team-leader roles, you mostly run what someone else has shaped. Perhaps you were involved in shaping it to some extent, but overall, your job was to run it and make sure the work got done.

> *When you become a leader of leaders, you become a shaper of the world around you.*

To do this, a core part of your role is about making sense of what's going on, determining why this is happening, and generating possibilities for where things should go next. You are also more involved in engaging others, especially your leadership team, and either convincing them that your narrative is the right one or working with them to create the narrative together. Let's look at another example.

James was the leader of a small team of three people. The team's job was to mass-produce CD recordings of live music, process the orders as they came in, and then dispatch the CDs out. James and his team could make minor adjustments to work processes, but on the whole James's job was to make sure the CD orders were filled correctly and dispatched. They were a small team, and it was a busy job.

I knew James at the time he had this position. Looking back, what was interesting was the way he talked in short sentences, often checking his phone for messages and calls. If a conversation went longer than ten to fifteen seconds, he would start looking around and fidgeting. He also moved fast – not just his legs when he was walking, but his whole body. His movements were short and sharp, and he was constantly in motion in some way. His mood always seemed rushed, urgent and task-focused.

James was very successful at this job, which we could label as that of a 'coordinator'. If we think about James's way-of-being in a job like this, it would probably look something like this:

EXPECTATIONS OF THE ROLE	LANGUAGE	MOOD/ EMOTIONS	BODY
Make sure daily orders are processed accurately and on time	Logistical, detailed, short-term, directive, operational (e.g., 'We must meet this deadline,' 'Why is that shipment delayed?' 'How am I going to get all this done today?' 'Why is John so slow?' 'I must check the daily status report')	Busy, feeling rushed, impatient, emotionally detached, on automatic pilot	Rapid movements, ready for immediate action, physically active, on-edge

Table 2. The way-of-being of a team coordinator

Eventually, James moved into a leader-of-leaders role. He was familiar with the concept of way-of-being, and worked to apply it in his transition to his new role. If you had known James before, when he was a team leader, you wouldn't recognise him as the same person in the way he approached his new role. Well, he of course still looks the same and is mostly still the same person, but he is different enough that you would notice.

The first difference you would observe about James is that he now moves slower than he used to. He sustains longer and wider-ranging conversations. He has a mood of curiosity and exploration. He is still focused and energised at work, but no longer quite as manic. His language is more exploratory and questioning. James has shifted his way-of-being.

Let's label this way-of-being that of the 'shaper'. In comparison to the coordinator way-of-being, the shaper's looks something more like this:

EXPECTATIONS OF THE ROLE	LANGUAGE	MOOD/ EMOTIONS	BODY
To shape the business to achieve growth in audience numbers and satisfaction, and ensure the future of the business in a changing market	Systemic, solution-oriented, building a strong team culture, thinking through complex problems and situations (e.g., 'How do we prepare the business for new technological opportunities?' 'What are the possibilities for launching a new service?' 'How can I develop the leadership capabilities of my direct-report	Calm, considerate, reflective, focused, open	Slower movements, more attentive in conversations, staying in one place for extended periods of time

Table 3. The way-of-being of a shaper (leader of leaders)

If James had not become a better observer of his own way-of-being, he would have continued doing his new senior leadership role in the same way. Straight away, you can see some of the big problems he would've hit. For starters, he wouldn't have spent the time to devote his slower and more considered focus towards the future and the whole system, which is a unique aspect of his new role. And if he wasn't doing that, no one else would be. Fortunately for James, he very quickly picked up on the need to shift his way-of-being.

So how did he do this?

Becoming an observer of your way-of-being

One of the practices that James developed during his transition to becoming a senior leader was to become a better observer of his own way-of-being. You may have heard the term 'self-awareness', which is a similar idea, but 'self-awareness' can be a little vague. The way-of-being model and the self-observation practices that we will look at below will give you a set of specific practices that you can apply at times of reflection and in the hurly-burly of leadership situations.

The action of observing your way-of-being is transformative. You'll be amazed at how different your experience becomes simply by more actively observing your way-of-being.

> 'We don't see the world as it is, we see it as we are.' – Anaïs Nin

Remember the way-of-being model with its three intersecting circles (Figure 4)? Here's how you can start to observe yourself across these three domains.

Language

Studies in the biology of cognition and philosophy of language have found that language doesn't just describe our experience, it also *generates* what we experience. The way we process an experience starts with the way we describe it to ourselves in our own heads.

The language we use as we speak with others also generates how we experience the world. Further, what we say out loud not only generates our experience, but also influences how others around us interpret their experience. This is an important insight for you as a leader to understand how you shape the mood and culture of your team and organisation.

The best starting point for becoming a better observer of your language is to capture what you are saying in your own head. Take a look at the statements below:

- 'I think my boss sees me as a bit weak on the numbers.'

- 'One of my peers is really out to discredit me.'

- 'I'm feeling anxious about the presentation I'm giving next week because the topic has become really political.'

This kind of self-talk is common. I'm pretty sure you've said similar things to yourself. Language like this activates your body for a false reality, so you may well experience a surge of anxiety-creating adrenaline from these situations that you've created in your own head.

If you use a lot of this kind of language in your self-talk, you can end up living in a mood of constant anxiety. So how do you stop yourself from engaging with these negative thoughts?

A simple first step is to start jotting down the talk that is going on in your head in different settings during your day. Become an observer of your language.

Emotions and moods

Emotions are feelings you have in response to a specific experience or interpretation of an experience. Moods are feelings you have over time that you can't seem to attach to a specific experience or interpretation of an experience. This can be another useful and powerful domain to observe.

A simple question to ask yourself regularly through the day is, 'What am I actually feeling right now?'

Just sense it. Don't make a judgement on it, just observe it. Another practice that can stop you from being too hard on yourself is to say to yourself, when you observe a feeling: 'Hmm, that's interesting.' That might sound funny, but it works. It will lead you back into a gentle, almost clinical observation of what you are feeling, rather than getting yourself down. It's also a good idea to note the various moods you find yourself in across your day, and to assign an appropriate label to them (for example: frustration, anxiety, satisfaction, resentment, resignation, anticipation).

Body

Although we have identified the body as the third domain of observation, this is the easiest to observe. We are biological creatures, and as such our bodies are designed to react very quickly and without conscious thought to perceptions of threat and danger. Back in the day, our nervous system would have been triggered by the thundering feet of a woolly mammoth; now, we can be just as triggered by the thumping footsteps of an angry boss. So once you get used to observing your body, it can give you the fastest access to what is going on in your way-of-being in all three domains.

The way you hold your body is called 'acture'. While I don't want to get too jargony, this is quite a useful term to keep in mind. It's a combination of two words – action and stature – which captures the idea that we give expression to our language and mood in the way we shape our stature for action. For example, if I am in a mood of anxiety, my acture is likely to be constrictive: my shoulders will tend to curve in, the muscles in my face and neck will tighten.

But the exciting thing is that the reverse is also true: if our emotion and mood can influence our acture, our acture can also influence our emotion and mood. So by making changes in my acture – perhaps relaxing the muscles around my mouth and eyes, pulling my shoulders back and looking up – I can start to shift my mood away from anxiety to one of curiosity and wonder.

A good place to start is to focus on your breathing. Don't change it straight away, just become aware of it. Then run a mental scan down your body. How are you holding your overall body shape? Are you slumped or upright? What is happening with your hands? Are your legs moving even though you're sitting down?

> *In taking these observations, you are not at all interested in how other people are interpreting your body shape. You are interested in how your body shape is contributing to your way-of-being.*

How to observe your way-of-being

It's important to capture your observations in a form that works naturally for you. Some people like to put pen to paper and write observations down in a journal; other people make notes on their phone, or use an app to talk it out and keep a recording. Whichever method you use, the important thing is to actively track your observations.

You can use the worksheet below to work out what is going on in your way-of-being by recording your current self-talk obser- vations, emotions/mood, and body in the first column. Then, in the second column, you can write down how you would like to adapt your way-of-being by changing your inner language, mood and body composition.

YOUR WAY-OF-BEING	CURRENT	FUTURE
Language (what and how you speak to yourself)		
Mood (the dominant mood of your day-to-day living)		
Body (the way you hold your body)		

Identifying patterns

As you start to collect these observations, you will start to see patterns and dynamics at work. For example, if you come out of a meeting that you experienced as tough and you're walking to your next meeting saying to yourself, 'People around here just don't get it, do they? They are such a pack of whining dumb arses.' Past interpretations will also factor in here – for instance, perhaps you've previously told yourself something like, 'Here we go again, it's all up to me to sort it out, as usual.'

In response to this self-talk, your body might tighten the muscles of your shoulders and face and activate some internal biochemistry that will charge you up so you can carry out this responsibility of having to cover for the dumb arses. You will experience all this as feelings of frustration, resentment, and even anger, and that is the mood that you will be in as you sit down in the next meeting. If you're unaware of this way-of-being, you run the risk that it will not only colour how you experience the people in the next meeting, but also the content of the meeting itself. If your body is tense and rigid, then this can literally constrict your cognition and inhibit creative thought: you may be more sceptical of new ideas, or might get too narrow-minded about what you accept as legitimate facts or valid proof. All this can have a significant impact on your business, as well as the management and leadership decisions you make.

Our mood sets the range of what we see as possible.

Adapting in the moment

The way-of-being you find yourself in each moment of each day as a leader determines how well you handle conversations, how open you are, and the decisions you make. The better you are at being an observer of your own way-of-being, the more you will be able to adapt your language, mood and body to shift into a more productive one. This will open new ways of interpreting your experience and expand your range of possibilities. Your experience of what is going on includes making sense of business situations and opening up new possibilities for strategies and actions.

In a world of constant change, complexity and ambiguity, being a leader of leaders who can actively adapt to new and emerging situations is impactful for both you and your organisation.

As a leader of leaders, your role is to shape the future of your teams and to influence the organisation beyond your own team. The future is all about possibilities, but your mood sets the range of what you can imagine is possible.

In this chapter we have explored how our mood is an important aspect of our way-of-being, and that it is generated through the language we use and the biological and structural responses of our bodies. If you're telling yourself that 'we are in a crisis and we must play it safe,' then you can find yourself in a mood of resignation. This immediately constricts the possibilities you can imagine and makes you less adaptable right at the time when openness and adaptiveness is what's needed.

While studying theory about leadership and management is very important, it can be difficult to draw on it or apply it in key moments where leadership is required. The practice of observing and adapting your way-of-being is a way to change your approach quickly when you don't have the time to sit down and think something through at a deeper level. Deeper and more conceptual reflection is also essential, but usually requires longer chunks of time away from day-to-day work.

Adapting your way-of-being to your new role as a senior leader is at the heart of your ability to make this big transition. You can start using this approach straight away.

> *Like any practice, the more you observe your way-of-being the more you will get the hang of it, and the more skilled you will become at not only observing it, but also shifting it.*

The impact of the department secretary's way-of-being

Stephen is the secretary of a large state government department. The first thing you notice when you meet Stephen is that he doesn't make himself the centre of the room, bustling around with an air of self-importance. His presence and influence don't come from him acting as if he's important – they emerge because of his way-of-being. If you were to use the model in Figure 4 to describe Stephen's way-of-being, you'd probably come up with something like this:

LANGUAGE	BODY	MOOD
Stephen speaks in everyday terms. He has a natural aversion to corporate buzzwords. He also speaks openly about the realities that his leadership team are facing. He doesn't gloss over challenges and difficulties, but names them in simple and straightforward language. Most of all, he listens more than he talks.	Stephen holds himself comfortably and upright, with an open stance. You could say his acture was casual and professional, not rigid and overly formal.	Stephen's mood is open, calm and quietly optimistic. He also brings a down-to-earth sense of humour that helps the team face challenges.

Overall, Stephen's way-of-being gives off a sense of perspective – an implicit assurance that whatever is going on around the organisation, and whatever the apparent concerns and threats, the team and the organisation will find a way forward. When you see Stephen and his leadership team in conversation, there is this same sense of relaxed openness. Difficult issues get talked about. Team members are clearly not afraid to ask questions and raise differing perspectives and ideas. Individuals in his leadership team are willing to be put on the spot in front of large gatherings of staff, even without prior notice. They adapt and collaborate to generate new organisation-wide strategies and rapid responses to community needs. In other words, you can call this the team 'culture'.

The organisational results, quality and innovation, and the timeliness of the services they deliver reflect this same way-of-being. The organisation is open, unpretentious, and deals with reality as it is. The senior leader's way-of-being is at the heart of the leadership team and the organisation.

IDEAS FOR ACTION

1. Start becoming an observer of your language, mood and acture. Keep a log of your observations to uncover patterns that indicate your way-of-being.

2. Pick a specific relationship or situation that is important to your success as a leader of leaders. Observe your way-of-being in that situation, and explore what the impact might be on your performance and the performance of your direct reports.

3. Start sharing the way-of-being idea with your direct-report leaders. It can become a useful framework for teams to reflect on performance and team effectiveness.

4. Learn more about way-of-being. Consult the 'Further reading' section at the back of this book for further reading.

QUESTIONS TO DIG DEEPER

1. What was going on in your way-of-being as you read this chapter? What mood did you find yourself in? What language was going through your head? How was this showing up in your body?

2. How would you describe your overall way-of-being in your role right now?

3. How is this way-of-being having an impact on your teams and your results?

4. What ideas come to mind about how you might like to adapt your way-of-being to be more productive and effective?

UP NEXT

In this chapter we explored the important idea of your way-of-being and its three dynamically interacting components: language, mood and body. We also learned how to become an observer of your way-of-being, and how you can use this to adapt your way-of-being to serve you well in your new role as a leader of leaders.

Chapter 4 will take you into the next phase: making sure you give yourself the promotion to leader of leaders in your own head.

4

Give yourself a promotion

ROSIE HAD JUST BEEN PROMOTED FROM A HUMAN RESOURCES business partner to the human resources director for a large operational division of the company she worked for. This meant Rosie also had a change of boss: now, she reported to the global head of human resources.

Rosie was a very smart, insightful and confident person in her mid-twenties. She was passionate not only about improving the business, but also about the business caring about its employees. Rosie always moved fast, and her language was short and to the point. She was used to having a lot of tasks to get done. One of the words she used a lot was 'management', as in, 'Management has to do something about such-and-such an issue,' or 'Management has to walk the talk.'

One day, she was in a team meeting with the global head of

human resources and the other senior leaders in the human resources team, who were her new peers. The team was engaged in a discussion about shaping the new human resources strategy for the whole company.

'Whatever else you do, management really must improve its focus on employee health and well-being,' said Rosie.

Her new boss, Matt, replied, 'Rosie, don't forget you are now management!'

Rosie stopped in her tracks. It was as if, with that one comment, Matt had broken through Rosie's learned assumptions about her role in the organisation and in the world. Rosie respected Matt, and knew his comment was coming from a good place. After the meeting broke up, she approached him.

'That comment really threw me,' she said. 'What are you getting at?'

'Rosie, I've noticed that you often talk about "management" as if you are a junior person in the organisation looking up at the leadership and making demands for stuff that you have no power to make happen,' replied Matt.

'Go on,' said Rosie, a slight smile of realisation starting to form.

'You are a divisional human resources director now. You are management,' Matt continued. 'Management isn't some other people – it's you. It's time to really understand that and own that. Then you will really start thinking and acting like the senior leader you now are.'

Although Rosie had been formally appointed to a leader-of-leaders role, with a new title, new location and a new level of pay, she had not yet given herself the promotion in her own head. She was continuing to work as if she were still in her business-partner role. Until her boss pointed that out, she was unaware that this would eventually get in the way of her succeeding in her new role. Rosie needed to give herself a promotion.

How you see yourself

We each walk around with a picture in our head of who we are and our place in the world. This image we have of ourselves can include a wide range of perspectives and roles – everything from 'I'm the tall one in the family,' to 'I must always be a good boy and not rock the boat,' right up to, 'I'm not in senior management, so I don't make big decisions.'

When it comes to our work, most people really identify closely with their role or profession. This is especially true of people who have invested many years in studying and training for their occupation. How we see ourselves drives how we interpret our experience, what we think we can do and say, and who we can have open conversations with. Changing how you see yourself is what giving yourself a promotion is all about.

> *Every change you make in your life begins*
> *with seeing yourself differently.*

Start by seeing yourself in a role a level above your new role. By doing so, you will stretch yourself and begin to see with the broader perspective of a leader.

What happens if you don't?

If you don't pay attention to this, you'll have no chance of succeeding in the role. It's as simple as that. Here are some of the ways you will stay stuck.

You'll keep functioning at the wrong level of work

The idea of 'level of work' was developed by Elliott Jacques. The gist of the concept is that different levels of leadership have different spans of responsibility, which require the person in the job to think at a more conceptual level and act in different ways with different people. If you keep functioning at your old level of work in your new role, it's like a carpenter who gets a job to build houses, but instead spends their days on site building furniture. Working at the wrong level means you end up working on the wrong things.

You'll micromanage your team leaders

You'll also find yourself doing that thing that everyone hates bosses doing: you'll micromanage people. Micromanagement is supervising people's work too closely, and giving them little or no scope to use their own initiative or ideas – or even their own brain!

No leader wakes up in the morning with the intention of going to work and micromanaging people. Most people who micromanage are unaware that they are doing it. But this is one of the most frustrating and demotivating experiences anyone can have at work. When you are on the receiving end of micromanagement, you can end up losing confidence in your abilities. One thing's for sure: you'll disengage from your boss and your work, and find yourself setting up a lot of job-search alerts.

> *If you stay stuck in your old ways, you are highly likely to micromanage the leaders that now report to you.*

You won't do the work of your new role

You will not put enough time and energy into the work that is unique to your role as a leader of leaders, because in your head you will be stuck in a different job. You'll be continually telling yourself and everyone around you that you don't have time do stuff like longer-term strategy and planning, innovation, and building the right culture. You'll never get around to doing the new job.

You won't be valued

You'll keep talking to the people at the level of work you have always worked at. You may find you spend too much time on your team members and not enough time with their leaders, your boss, and the wider web of working relationships. Lack of attention to this wider web of relationships is fatal. If you keep doing the same job or even working in the same way you used to, your efforts won't be seen as valuable. Different things are valued at this new level of work.

> *So, if you keep doing stuff that isn't valued in your new role, then you won't be valued!*

Five steps to your promotion

Fortunately, giving yourself a promotion is not as weird as it sounds. These five steps will help to shift your perspective and also your day-to-day practices as a leader. These steps are vital in your early days of becoming a leader of leaders, and they will remain important foundations for your ongoing career in senior leadership roles.

It's a good idea to adopt a practice in which you review how you are going with each of these steps at the end of every week. This will help you to see when you are falling back into familiar but less effective practices, and will encourage you as you see yourself making these important changes.

1. Focus on the unique value of your role

In your new senior leadership role, you will find that you have more scope to shape how you use your time. Sure, you'll still have stuff that you just must do: requests to sign off on, material to review, and work processes from your broader organisation that every leader in the place must adhere to. The danger of this is that, even though you now have more power to shape what you work on and how you work on it, you can slip into your old style of doing work that isn't important in your new role, or worse, doing the work of others.

That's why the first step in giving yourself a promotion is to work out what the unique value of your role is.

Here's the question:

> *What is the value that this job brings that no other job brings?*

Although the answer to this question will depend on the context of your specific role, what the leader-of-leaders role does that no other job does is build and sustain the system that your team works in. Other people might think about this from time to time, but it's your job to actually *do* it. You need to hover over the whole system that you're responsible for and make sure that all the elements are working well together to achieve the outcomes the business requires. No other role carries this responsibility.

2. Shape your time

In your leader-of-leaders role, you will find that you have more power and opportunity to shape what you do, how you do it, and what order you do it in. Leaders have two limited resources: time and energy.

In your previous role your time was often structured for you, with set meetings to attend and set tasks to get done. Also, tasks were often channelled your way and determined by the workflow. Your job was to make sure it all got done, either by your team or by you yourself. In your new role, this happens less – sometimes a lot less.

> *Give yourself the promotion by actively shaping your months, weeks and days.*

You need to shape your time to make sure you are paying attention to the unique contribution of your role.

3. Mind your language

Also, make sure to mind your language! You've surely heard people rushing around saying things like 'I have to go to that meeting,' or 'I have no choice but to stay late and finish this.' This is the language of *external focus*, which is the notion that you have very little choice and must go along with what other people want. This kind of language will generate a mood of resignation '(I have no choice, and there is no point in trying to do what I want or what's important to me and my role'), and will often lead to feelings of anxiety and stress.

> As a leader of leaders, it's important that you are mostly in a mood that is open to possibility, action and choice.

You decide which meetings you go to. *You* choose to work on certain tasks and not others. If your boss calls a meeting and you are expected to be there, you could still not go if *you* think your time could be better spent on other tasks. Depending on your boss and the nature of the meeting, this might matter a lot or not at all. Even if you are choosing to go to the meeting because you want to keep your job, you are still exercising choice and strengthening your work focus. The important thing is that you use language that generates a sense of choice and empowerment rather than drudgery.

4. Manage your energy

The other resource you need to manage carefully is your energy. Being a leader of leaders comes with different ebbs and flows of intensity. Not all aspects of your role are of equal importance, so you want to make sure you are at your best for crucial decision points, efficiently understanding important information and demanding conversations when needed. You need mental, emotional and physical energy at these important points.

So, how do you look after your energy? The first point is to remember that you are human, and that you only have a finite amount of energy each day. Here's some other important things to remember:

- Physical health and well-being are a major support for our mental and emotional energy. Keep fit and get regular good sleep.

- Allow for downtime and breaks. If you know you have an intense, emotionally demanding meeting coming up, then allow a fifteen- or thirty-minute break afterwards. You may be thinking, 'You're kidding, how can I do that?' but you *can* do it. You might just be afraid of what you imagine other people will think about you. It's most likely your brain will need some recovery time. At least schedule yourself to complete more relaxed work to follow the meeting.

- Have a finite number of hours you'll normally work in

a day. There has been a lot of research that working long hours results in a rapid decline in productivity. We all know that moment while working on something when we suddenly realise that we've just been staring at the computer screen for ten minutes or going over and over the same stuff and not really getting it. Also, setting boundaries for your day helps you to not waste time. Some days things will go crazy, and you may decide to go with that. But as a rule, there is very little productivity happening when you push beyond the eight- or nine-hour mark in a day.

5. Look and feel

The final step in giving yourself a promotion is more subjective, but quite powerful – namely, how do you look and feel when you are a leader of leaders? This is not about how other people judge your appearance, but rather about the changes that are important to make so that you feel like yourself in a new role. Below are some things to think about; there may be others that apply specifically to you and your new role.

Dress and appearance

What style of clothes and general 'look' might help you feel like you are now a leader of leaders? More casual? More formal? Remember, this is not about trying to conform to some external standard, but rather about how *you* want to feel. Some people opt to change their wardrobe and get a fresh new look. This can be a very powerful way for you to signal to yourself that you are moving into a new phase of your career.

Objects

Physical objects matter. They are signals to us and our own body that we are different from who we used to be. What new tools or accessories will help you feel like you are now in a bigger role? Perhaps you might acquire a new device, the latest laptop, or a new briefcase.

Mood refresh

Starting a new, different and bigger role is a great time to actively refresh your mood towards your work and career. Even the most motivated people get stale, bored, and feel like they are just going through the motions.

You can refresh your mood in lots of different ways. While taking a break and getting away is always a great way to do this, making day-to-day changes will have a more lasting impact. Try some of these ideas:

- Get to your workplace by a different form of transport or take a different route. Perhaps you have always driven to work, so try catching a bus sometimes, or even walking (which will allow you to get exercise at the same time).

- Go to a different café or series of different cafés for your daily coffee.

- Take short breaks to do nothing. Most roles can be frenetic, so simply going outside for even five minutes, looking up at the sky and walking around the block can refresh your perspective and mood.

Whatever you choose to do, remember that this is all about changing your routines so that you are physically doing different things in a different environment. This can be a turning point as you realise that your mood is yours to adapt and shape.

Rituals and ceremonies

Ancient and indigenous societies place a great emphasis on the importance of ritual and ceremony to mark significant life events and turning points. We have some of these in the modern world of work, even if we tend not to think of them as such. Farewell drinks are a good example, but even something as simple as cleaning your workspace can have an important ritualistic quality to it.

A ritual or ceremony that helps you leave behind your old role and promote yourself into your new role can be a powerful method of adaption. You don't even have to tell anyone else about it! For example, I once burned some documents and gave away some reference books to tell myself that I was moving on from an old way of life and way-of-being.

You are where you should be

As you give yourself the promotion, you will find you start to feel like you are where you should be. You will feel legitimate in your new role as a leader of leaders. If you use the five-step approach above, you will start to sense the shift in yourself almost right away. Like learning anything new, the more you practice, the more you will sense yourself adapting. You will start to see tangible growth in your new role.

> *You will start to feel like you belong in the role.*

Any new job feels strange at first. It demands different things of us, and we must learn to work in different ways with different people. By giving yourself the promotion, you will feel like you belong in the role because you will leave behind your old ways of working and start to really do your new job. You get more in flow, and feel more natural.

As you start to feel more legitimate as a leader of leaders, you can also be yourself more. Instead of feeling like you are pretending, you will discover the natural 'you' in this role. Senior leadership roles can be done in lots of different ways. In fact, the more you 'do you' in the role, the more impact and influence you will have as a leader.

As your natural flow and sense of legitimacy grow, your confidence in various interactions will grow as well.

Because you have done the work of giving yourself the promotion, you will feel less self-conscious. By doing this, you'll bring more of your ideas and thoughts forward. You'll have more impact.

One of the exciting things about moving into a leader-of-leaders role is that you have a much wider span of influence and more power to do good things. I still remember the feeling of exhilaration in my first few months as a leader of leaders. Sure, at times I felt nervous and even overwhelmed, but it was also exciting to start to see the bigger picture and to imagine what might be possible.

Sometimes in the early months of your new role, you will feel uncertain, and may even feel like an impostor.

The best way to not let these feelings stunt your growth in the role is to give yourself the promotion.

From tongue-tangle to senior leader

When Jodie first started going into meetings with senior leaders, she would get tongue-tied when she had to speak. Even though she was normally an articulate professional, she would stumble and lose the plot in these high-level meetings. Jodie found this frustrating, and began to think she would have to accept the level she was at for the rest of her career. Something inside of her just went to water once the spotlight landed on her.

Jodie began to work with the idea of giving herself the promotion. Because a lot of her struggle seemed to be physical and unconscious, she focused on her look and feel in particular in order to gain confidence. Before and even during meetings with senior leaders, she would say things in her head like, 'I am a senior leader in this place, and I belong here.'

She also created a ritual that only she knew about. After she sat down in a meeting, she would make subtle adjustments to her body posture. Some of these shifts were things like sitting more upright, and holding her shoulders back and her neck straighter. Jodie found that this focus on look and feel generated a sense of confidence and presence within herself in meeting situations.

Quite quickly after she started instituting these changes, the tongue-tied stumbling stopped. Jodie was able to deliver her presentations clearly and concisely and engage in robust discussion with senior leaders. In the following six months, she was successful in her application for a senior manager role as a leader of leaders. And the starting point of it all was giving herself the promotion.

IDEAS FOR ACTION

1. Write in one sentence the unique value of your new leader-of-leaders role.

2. Write down the top three most important activities that will deliver this unique value.

3. Look at your monthly calendar and allocate time to do these activities.

4. Design a ritual or ceremony that will help you give yourself the promotion.

QUESTION TO DIG DEEPER

1. What do you sometimes catch yourself thinking and saying that might show that you have not given yourself the promotion?

2. Imagine that you are in a role one level above your new one. How would you want to feel in that role?

3. Which ways of thinking and work practices do you want to leave behind now that you have given yourself the promotion?

UP NEXT

In this chapter we looked at how important it is to give yourself a promotion, and how this impacts the way you see yourself in the world.

Chapter 5 introduces the core practice for leading other leaders: giving space for your leaders to lead while still ensuring they are heading in the right direction. In this chapter, you'll learn how to make sandboxes!

5

Create sandboxes for your leaders

DANNI IS AN ENERGETIC, BUBBLY AND ENTHUSIASTIC LEADER. In the morning when she arrives at the office, she always announces her arrival with a big 'Good morning!' and goes around to greet each team. She remembers everyone's birthday, and personally leads the birthday-afternoon teas for each person. She loves to fix problems, and is always happy to jump in with an answer whenever anyone is struggling with something.

Yet despite all Danni's effort and energy, her staff engagement scores were slowly but surely declining. She genuinely couldn't understand what was going on. 'What more can I do for them!' she would often exclaim in frustration.

Danni's approach had served her well as a team leader, and she is a very likeable person, but she didn't realize that she was unintentionally driving her direct reports crazy. In her enthusiasm, she was forever butting in on conversations that the team leaders were having with their teams, jumping in front of computers to solve technical problems for team members, and contradicting the decisions of her team leaders.

But those were only the minor issues. The big problem was that Danni gave almost no power to her team leaders. Most decisions had to come to her for approval. She addressed the whole team on issues that only concerned one team, or even just a few people. Thinking she was being a great support to her team leaders, Danni was involved in all performance and development reviews. If improvement feedback had to be given, Danni insisted on doing it herself because she didn't think the team leaders were skilled enough to handle those situations.

Danni was frustrated by her team leaders because she thought they lacked motivation and initiative. She felt they were a sullen lot, moping around or just sitting at their computers doing processing work. 'Why can't they at least put a smile on their faces?' she would ask herself.

Then, some of her most effective team leaders started to leave. Themes started to emerge from the exit interviews about micromanagement, lack of support for team leaders, and systemic problems that never seemed to get fixed. A restructure came along, and Danni's role was made redundant. She left to find another role in a different organisation.

Let me reiterate that Danni is not a bad person, and not even a bad leader. In fact, she is a genuinely caring, highly team-oriented leader. But unfortunately, she couldn't make the transition to become a leader of leaders. Her career in the organisation derailed because she didn't build sandboxes for her leaders.

> *You need to create space for your leaders to, well, lead!*

The work sandbox

In work-culture terms, a 'sandbox' is a defined space with clear boundaries that contains a range of tools and resources that the people in the sandbox are free to use as they like. The sandbox is a great metaphor for this important practice, which is one of the key aspects of being a leader of leaders.

Your team leaders *must* have a sandbox – otherwise, they aren't leaders. Danni had not yet learned how essential it is to create space for her leaders to lead. As a result, her good intentions generated frustration, anger and disengagement – the complete opposite of what she was genuinely striving to create.

Just like a child's sandbox, a leader's sandbox has some essential features. These include:

Boundaries. You must clearly set the limits within which the leader can exercise their leadership. Clear boundaries spark energy, motivation and action by leaders because they know what they can and can't do. Clear boundaries are liberating.

Sand. You need to give your leaders control over some resources. The leader must have the authority to decide on the allocation and use of at least some resources. This includes the two most important organisational resources: people and money.

Toys and tools. Your team leaders must have access to and authority over the allocation and use of equipment.

Design rights. Human beings get a deep feeling of satisfaction and meaning from shaping the world around them. Part of the fun of being a child in a sandbox is that you can build whatever you want within the boundaries and parameters of the sandbox. Having the freedom and authority to design (or redesign) how work is done is an import aspect of being a leader. If you want to generate strong engagement and motivation from your leaders, make sure you give them some scope to design and redesign work systems and processes.

All these elements are necessary components to make important things happen and to achieve outcomes that matter.

> *Creating and sustaining sandboxes is essential if you want to unlock the power of your leadership team.*

Why sandboxes really matter

Creating and sustaining sandboxes is at the heart of being a leader of leaders. This is because it's the leaders that report to you who are the main generators of great outcomes. Sandbox-building is the main difference between your previous role and your new senior leadership role.

If you don't create and maintain these sandboxes, your direct reports will become unsatisfied leaders doing professional-contributor work. Apart from this being a waste of money and talent, disgruntled leaders can also spread the bad vibe to their staff via a trickle-down effect. A dissatisfied leader is not an isolated problem: they fester and eat away at the culture and morale of the broader team. Remember, they are being paid to lead, so it's more than okay to expect them to lead, and to see their leadership practices as a core part of their performance in their job.

One question I like asking of senior leaders is, 'How many people report to you?' Their answers are telling. Often, they will say the number of the total team ('Oh, about eighty people'). This answer tells me that the person is still being a leader of individuals, and is most likely not building sandboxes for leaders.

As a leader of leaders, your direct reports are the people you are leading. It's not your job to lead every single one of the individual contributors within your wider team – that's the job of your leaders. This is an essential mind shift that you need to make: you lead the leaders; the leaders lead the individuals. It may not always be that simple in the hurly-burly of getting stuff done, but it's important that you recognise this as your default setting.

And if you feel that some situations do require you to breach that fundamental principle, you need to understand the significance of that breach and know that you will likely need to do some cleaning up afterwards. For example, if you decide that you need to intervene in the work of one of your teams and perhaps even contradict a decision made by that team's leader, it's vital that you have a follow-up conversation with the leader as soon as possible. This is a big deal for them, and it should be for you too.

This is how you make your job doable. This is how you get the time and energy to focus on the other aspects of your role that won't get done unless you do them – particularly the important work we'll cover in the next chapter.

> *Creating sandboxes is the only way to sustain your own energy and motivation in a leader-of-leaders role.*

You can't do everything on your own. It's impossible. If you don't give priority to sandbox-building you will end up working ridiculously long hours, plus evenings and weekends. And even then you won't get through all that has to get done. You will burn out. How long this takes will depend on how determined you are: it may take three months or it might take eighteen months, but in the end, you *will* burn out.

Barriers to creating sandboxes

If consciously and actively creating sandboxes for your leaders is so important, then it just makes sense that every leader of leaders should make it a top priority, right? And yet every week, leaders I'm coaching try to explain to me all the reasons why they haven't got around to building them. All of them agree that it's a great idea, but just 'not right now'. Here are some of the reasons they typically give:

'It's quicker to do it myself.'

This might appear to be true for a specific task at first – and, if you don't mind doing everything yourself and working 24/7, then it's a good approach. When you have been a technical expert for a long time, it can initially be a real challenge to hold off from leaping in and doing a task that you know you're good at rather than letting the person who is now responsible for this figure it out for themselves. Later in this chapter, we'll take you through some practical steps you can use to start building sandboxes with your leaders while still making sure the work gets done how it needs to get done.

'It won't be done right.'

This may be true, but then again, it might not be! Quite often, the first time someone tries to do something they haven't done before, they don't get it right. But then again, you probably weren't born being able to do the work you mastered previously, so you should now give it to one of your leaders for them to figure out. You learned, and other people will too.

'It won't be done as well as I would do it.'

This might sound a bit like 'It won't be done right,' but it's different in a very important way. When a leader is talking about getting something done 'right', this implies that there is only one way for something to be done. Typically, a leader has a set view on how something 'should' be done, when in reality there are several equally valid methods that will achieve the same result. A fresh set of eyes can often discover better ways to do things.

'I don't have time.'

This is a bit like saying you don't have time to be a leader! Creating sandboxes is crucial to a leader's job. If you don't make time to create sandboxes, then you will fail, burn out, or both. As we will see later, sandbox-building is something that can be done gradually, in small, manageable chunks that don't interfere with your day-to-day responsibilities.

'What if the leader ends up doing a better job than me and I lose my job?'

Thankfully, this particular excuse seems to have died out, or at least gone underground. Said out loud, it sounds a bit paranoid, right? But it can still show up in your moods and emotions in the shape of insecurity or anxiety when you get the sense that your direct report is smarter than you in some way. But instead of being afraid that your leaders are better leaders than you, dance around and be happy about it! Having brilliant direct reports makes your life as a leader so much easier. In fact, the more your team grows in capability and performance, the more your reputation as a leader will be enhanced.

Designing and building sandboxes is important, but not urgent. The thing is, there is never an easy 'quiet' time to get into designing and building sandboxes, but the more you hang on to excuses like the above, the more urgent it will become. The risk is that, by then, your new role will have gotten away from you and it will be too late to turn it around.

Designing sandboxes

If it's so important to create sandboxes for your leaders, how do you do this? In this section we are going to look at the principles that guide strong sandbox-building, explore an example of a sandbox build, and determine what is important to sustain the strength and integrity of the sandbox.

Your sandbox should be a triangle, because the strongest shape in the world is the triangle. It is at the core of building: if you climb into the roof of a house, you will see that its rafters are constructed in the shape of triangles. Just think of the Egyptian pyramids.

> *Leadership sandboxes build strength and*
> *energy into the organisation of your team.*

The three sides of the triangle are the three parameters that are agreed upon between you and each of your leaders. Those parameters are a) responsibility, b) authority, and c) accountability. As you can see from Figure 5 below, the sandbox is an equilateral triangle, with each side the same length. This means that each parameter is in equal balance with the other two parameters. It's a good idea to document the details of the sandbox parameters so that both you and your leaders are clear on the limits of the sandbox.

Figure 5. The Sandbox Triangle®
The Sandbox Triangle® is a trademarked model of Being Leaders Pty Ltd.

Let's look at what each of these means and how the balance works.

Responsibility

The responsibility parameter defines what your team leaders must achieve. For example, one of your leaders might be heading the team that's responsible for collating monthly financial reports. In their responsibility parameter, then, you would write down the specific outcomes they are responsible for achieving. If it's important, you would also include quality requirements and timeframes.

What is included in the responsibility parameter can vary a lot depending on what industry you work in. Some are quite detailed, while others are more of a direction or goal that the leader is responsible for achieving, and there may be a lot of scope and discretion for the leader to decide what the outcomes look like.

Accountability

The term 'accountability' means to 'give an account of', or to tell the story of what you have achieved and what you may not have achieved. It has become a bit of a loaded word in many organisations, with the implication that being held accountable is the same as getting into trouble. Sometimes it's even used as a threat ('I'll make you accountable!').

For the accountability parameter, by contrast, you and your team leader will simply agree on how you will both be able to gauge that the things the leader is responsible for have been achieved. For some leader roles this is straightforward: for instance, in our example from above of the team that is responsible for producing reports, the accountability parameter could be as simple as delivering reports that meet the required standards and timelines. But for other leader roles, accountability parameters may not be quite as clearcut. For example, in a research and development function, the accountability parameter may have a broader range of things to look at that would show progress towards achieving areas of responsibility, rather than a clear and measurable result.

Authority

The third parameter of the leader's sandbox is authority. This is about specifying what power the leader has to do a range of things, such as:

- How much of the organisation's money can they spend without getting approval from you?

- What decisions can they make about hiring, firing and managing performance without getting approval from you?

- What business decisions can they make to change work systems and processes?

There is no right or wrong when it comes to how much specific authority to give your leader, but there are two useful principles that can help you determine the extent of their autonomy:

1. The authority parameter must be generous enough for the leader to balance their authority with the responsibility and accountability they have. There is nothing more frustrating and inefficient than not being able to approve decisions that you are responsible for.

2. Give your leaders as free a hand as you can to achieve what they must achieve. For example, you might decide to give your reporting leader authority to spend up to 5,000 dollars a month on staff costs for reward and recognition without needing approval from you. You might also give them the authority to recruit replacement team members in line with budget headcount, and require them to bring you in on the final interview process.

> The Sandbox Triangle® of responsibility, accountability and authority is a great framework for creating spaces for your leaders to lead while still ensuring that they work towards agreed outcomes within agreed boundaries.

The key point to remember is that the three parameters must be equal. The leader's accountability must align with their responsibility, and they need to have sufficient authority to enable them to allocate resources and effort to achieve their responsibilities.

Gradually growing bigger sandboxes

Some people who are new to the leader-of-leaders role will initially be reluctant to build sandboxes for their direct reports. And behind that reluctance is a legitimate concern, along the lines of: 'How can I create sandboxes for my leaders and still make sure the important stuff gets done properly and on time?'

When senior leaders first start to engage with the idea of sandboxes, they often assume that you go from no sandbox to a huge, autonomous sandbox in one go. They then get rightly concerned that their reports won't be able to cope with the change, the important stuff won't get done, and chaos will descend. But you don't have to build the sandbox all at once – instead, you can gradually delegate a balance of responsibility, accountability and authority in a phased approach, like this:

Phase 1: the leader is authorised to investigate/ review a function or project and then report back to you to confirm their understanding

This gives the leader a chance to get their head around the new task, and gives you the opportunity to check how well they understand the work and what's required. You can also see how much they are looking at things as a leader, not as a professional contributor.

Phase 2: the leader is authorised to investigate/ review and make recommendations to you

Often there are aspects of a function or project that require closer attention. Again, this step gives the leader the opportunity to think about their approach to the work, and you'll want to see them considering leadership aspects in their recommendations as well. It also gives you the chance to see what approach they are going to take without letting them loose too soon.

Phase 3: the leader is authorised to investigate/ review and act, then report back to you

Now that you have the evidence that they understand the function or project and how they are going to approach it as a leader, it's time to let them get into it. You can also do this step gradually by letting the leader act on some initial aspects of the work, and then hand over the rest when you can see they are going well. You'll want to make sure that they are paying attention to the leadership dimensions.

Phase 4: the leader is authorised to act on an ongoing basis and report back to you on a regular basis (weekly or monthly)

The first three phases will give you a good sense of how the leader is getting along. This takes a lot of the anxiety out of sandbox-building. Once you can see that they are on a roll, you can leave them to it and set up a regular reporting process.

The idea is that you don't progress to the next phase until you and the leader are confident enough to move on. How long it takes to work through the phases depends on the scale of the function or project. For a relatively simple project, you might work through the four phases in two days, whereas a bigger and more complex project might require you to spread the phases across three months.

Gradually building sandboxes with your leaders also creates a systematic leadership development experience for them that is integrated into their work responsibilities. Sandbox-designing, -building and -reviewing is a perfect opportunity to coach your leaders on leadership mindsets and practices. The phased approach also gives you a good way to track their growth and development as a leader.

Maintaining the sandbox

Setting up your leaders' sandboxes is not a one-time event. Once you have worked through the three parameters for each of your leaders, it's important to review the triangle every three to six months, or if circumstances change dramatically. While it's useful to have the details of each parameter written down and agreed upon, the higher value lies in the ongoing conversation between you and your leaders.

You also need to make sure you honour and respect their position as a leader. Don't breach their triangle: if you are concerned about something going on in their team, never deal with it directly unless it carries an immediate safety or well-being risk.

Your leaders are an untapped resource of leadership power just waiting to be brought online. The time and energy you use in working with your leaders to create their sandboxes will pay off tenfold in the motivational energy, ideas, initiatives, problem-solving and workflow Improvement that they will bring. Overall, leaders underutilise the strengths, talent, willingness and energy of the people who work for them, and this is a particular waste when it comes to your leaders. Both individually and collectively, our people have the potential to contribute far more than we often imagine.

> *Working with your leaders to create and continuously refine their sandboxes will really set your whole team up for growing success.*

As individual leaders start to lead their teams, engagement and performance will actively take off. Leaders who know they have space to lead will engage with more energy and bring more of their strengths into play. This has a powerful ripple effect on their team members, which will lift performance and engagement across the whole team. Responsiveness and innovation will grow, and their teams will perform with greater care, speed and quality.

Creating sandboxes also means that you will start to develop the next generation of leaders. Leaders who have been given a clear space to play in also have a clear space to learn and grow as leaders. They get to make real decisions about people, money, strategies and processes. They have a space to exercise their leadership muscles and make them stronger as a result. Yes, they will make mistakes – just like you did, and still do. But the best way to learn is always by doing.

In turn, your job as a leader of leaders will become more satisfying, and you will feel more like you can do it. Leaders of leaders that get hold of the sandbox idea start to experience a sense of having more time and space themselves. You might even have a weird feeling of guilt as you find that you are less caught up in sorting out the day-to-day stuff, but don't worry.

> *You will have plenty of things to fill the time, but they will be things that are important to your role as a leader of leaders.*

Activating leaders and getting home on time

Remember Amani from Chapter 1, who was stuck in the office late on a Friday night? Her story didn't end there: in fact, it was through those moments of emotional pain and despair that Amani realised that her old ways of working wouldn't cut it in her new role, and she became determined to find a totally different way to work. Sometimes, pain is a great motivator!

When Amani heard about the idea of creating sandboxes for her direct reports, she leaped on it. Her leaders had been her major problem since she moved into her new role. She was frustrated by what she interpreted as their unwillingness to take responsibility and their daily habit of passing decision-making up to her.

Amani immediately set out to create sandboxes for her leaders. Using the triangle of responsibility, accountability and authority, she worked with each leader to carve out a sandbox that matched their area of responsibility. While some of her five leaders loved the change and embraced the freedom and power of their sandbox, not all of them were happy at first. It turned out that a couple of them quite liked the fact that they got paid to lead, but could just send the hard stuff up to Amani. But now that Amani had established clear expectations for all her leaders, and laid the plans for an ongoing design of the sandbox that would incorporate feedback from her reports, she was equipped with a framework that would highlight the leaders who had great potential and were now released to lead, and reveal those that were reluctant to live up to their leadership responsibilities.

Over a three-to-four-month period, Amani was able to reduce her involvement in day-to-day operational work and shift her focus to influencing for integration. Her immediate boss and directors noticed the rapid change in how Amani was showing up, as well as the improving performance of her team. More importantly, she got to go home and have that Friday-night dinner with her partner.

IDEAS FOR ACTION

1. Take a moment to review how you are currently working with each of your team leaders. Use the Sandbox Triangle® to map out what each of their sandboxes would look like.

2. Have a conversation with each of your team leaders about the ideas in this chapter, and get their views on how their current sandbox is working for them.

3. Authority is often the one parameter that leaders neglect. Take a closer look at how clear the authority component is working for each of your team leaders. Is it enough, too much, or too little?

4. Review your current list of things you must get done. What is one activity or project that you could move into one of your team leader's sandboxes? What difference would that make to your workload and focus? Often, team leaders love the opportunity to develop through doing different and more complex work.

QUESTIONS TO DIG DEEPER

1. What feelings came up for you as you read this chapter?

2. What thoughts did you have about the idea of sandboxes?

3. What language and assessments might get in the way of you really giving the sandbox idea a go? For example, a common objection to the sandbox idea is that it's quicker and easier to do it yourself. If you think that way, then you will always be stuck doing that work and never have the space to grow into a leader of leaders.

4. What possibilities for you and your new role can you imagine if you really put sandboxes into practice?

UP NEXT

This chapter took you through the concept of sandboxes, why these are essential in leading other leaders, how to set them up and how to maintain them.

Chapter 6 expands your possibilities even further by looking at the other vital part of your new role, which is to make sure the work of your teams stays connected with the organisation's bigger goals.

6

Influence to integrate

PAUL HAD BEEN A VERY SMART CONTRIBUTOR, AND THEN A successful leader of small, rapidly deployed project teams. But his new senior leadership role was becoming overwhelming and frustrating.

Paul had recently been appointed to the biggest role of his career, as director of shared services for a large scientific research organisation. At first, Paul thought that success in his role was all about driving tight project management. He was very good at this, and his great strength in precision project management had brought him great success.

But in his new leadership role, he was not getting the support of his peers on the executive team. This meant project timelines were blowing out, and he and his team were getting the blame. Paul had tried to push through by producing detailed project plans with clear timeframes so his executive colleagues could organise their teams. But instead of getting commitment and support, he was criticised for his 'pushy' style. Some of his peers became disengaged, and became too busy to meet with him or didn't review project plans by the due dates he had mapped out.

Fortunately, Paul is very open to unlearning and relearning, so he took advantage of some coaching support to help make the necessary changes to his way-of-being and leadership practices. His goal was to connect the efforts of his team to the whole organisation. Paul focused on two of his peers in particular, who were the executive leaders of the two biggest divisions.

The most significant impact of Paul taking the same project-management approach that he was accustomed to using was that he unintentionally alienated himself and his reporting leaders from the executives leading the biggest parts of the business. Now, rather than producing detailed project plans and sending them out, he listed some basic project parameters and then spent time in genuine co-design with his peers to better understand their requirements and workflows. This helped to create an action plan that would work for everyone.

Beyond that, Paul set up regular catch-ups with his peers with the goal of deepening his understanding of the strategies and plans in each part of the organisation. When his peers voiced criticism about the service levels they received from Paul's team, Paul worked at listening to and understanding their concerns rather than simply leaping to the defence of his teams.

Over a six-month period, Paul began to win the engagement and support of his fellow leaders. The colleague who headed up the biggest division still found Paul's style a bit blunt at times, but now felt that Paul better understood the priorities of his division, and appreciated his positive and constructive intentions.

Paul also realised that he tended to cushion his direct reports and their teams from some of the harsh feedback of his peers, and decided to not do that anymore. From this point on, he immediately passed on all feedback to his team leaders, positive and negative. At first this was troubling for them, but over the months they realised that it was better to know what people were really thinking about them so that they could keep improving their services to the organisation.

Paul had realised that detailed project plans and forceful project management were not going to be enough to ensure his team's important work was integrated into the flow of the organisation. What had ensured his career success to date was about to derail his future, and he understood that he had to become a leader across the organisation and a supportive colleague of his peer executive leaders. He had to put more time and energy into influencing to integrate.

The teams you now lead don't exist in isolation. They are one part of a much larger system both in and beyond the organisation. As a leader of leaders, your focus must shift and expand.

> *You are now the representative, the custodian, the advocate and the translator of your team, the work they do, and the outcomes they deliver to others.*

Your team ecosystem

You are most likely now a member of a senior leadership team. This team is just as important as your own team, and in some ways more so. While advocating for your team is admirable, it's easy to slip into the trap of thinking that leadership is all about supporting 'your people'. Remember, you are now part of a wider leadership group that includes fellow leaders who also report to your boss in a formally structured sense. Your success as a senior leader in the broader organisation will now be determined more by how you engage with the other people at your level, and the culture you develop with them.

> *Now it's more important to be able step back from your teams and their work so you can look at them from the outside in.*

To see your team from a more objective standpoint as one component of the broader organisation is important for coordinating your efforts. You need to become a two-way channel: not only are you promoting the objectives and work of your team to the broader organisation and beyond, but you are also channelling the formal and informal performance feedback and reputation of your teams back to your direct reports. You don't help your leaders by patronisingly 'protecting' them, but rather by bringing the reality of their broader environment into their field of vision.

Part of this reality emerges from engaging with leaders in other areas of the organisation, and partners or customers outside the organisation. An effective thing you can do is to continually educate your leaders and the team about what is going on in this wider environment. There are lots of creative ways you can do this.

> *Integrating the work of your team into the current and future work environment is the responsibility of the leader of leaders.*

It can also be an interesting aspect of your leader-of-leaders role, and open you up to further development in your role and even future career opportunities.

Isolation leads to irrelevance

Influencing to integrate is tricky, because it's not necessarily an urgent priority. If you don't do it today or even this week, life will still go on. But it's easy to get caught up in the day-to-day and not put enough time and energy into this aspect of your new role. You must be disciplined and give this work the priority it requires over the medium term. If you don't integrate your team with the wider system and context, then you and your team are exposed to risks.

Risk 1: Miss the subtle shifts

You and your team fail to keep up with informal and gradual shifts in customer expectations, organisational mood and culture. This is the stuff that isn't in the official emails, or even presented in meetings. It's not that people are deliberately hiding anything – rather, it's more that you start to miss these emerging themes and movements. What this means is that you can end up like a tourist in a foreign country who doesn't have a grasp on its language and customs. It may be subtle, but in some important ways, you and your team are starting to not 'click' with the rest of the organisation.

Risk 2: Become disconnected

If you and your team miss enough of these subtle shifts, you can gradually become disconnected from the main strategy and flow of the organisation. This often first shows itself in little moments, such as when you misread a cue in a meeting, or one of your leaders gets wound up about an issue that isn't that important in the larger scheme of things. This doesn't happen overnight, but your connection can erode unless you, as a leader of leaders, work to maintain it.

Risk 3: Internal focus

You and your team can drift into too much internal focus. You start spending too much time and energy on relationships in your team, what's not working, how you irritate each other, and what's wrong with the rest of the organisation (which, of course, just 'doesn't understand' what your team is going through). You start moaning about other teams and how they seem to be ignoring you and keeping you out of the loop. In other words, your team will start to have an internal reference point rather than an external reference point.

Risk 4: Fail to collaborate

You can start to miss the opportunities to genuinely collaborate with other leaders and other teams across the organisation. Because you are becoming disconnected, missing the cues, and getting too internally focused, you can't identify areas of improvement and collaboration. This failure comes at a high cost to the organisation, as it's in these kind of cross-organisational collaborations that innovation is born. It will still happen, but you won't be a part of it. And you won't realise it until it's too late.

Risk 5: Get a negative reputation

As the previous risks start to materialise, they combine to gradually erode the reputation of you and your team. Everyone, and certainly every leader, has a reputation in your organisation. People *do* talk about you behind your back – it's just what humans do. If you are not paying enough attention to influencing to integrate, other leaders and contributors will most likely say less nice things about you and your team. One of the most disturbing experiences as a senior leader is to find out that your peers or other leaders in the organisation are starting to bypass you and your team.

Risk 6: Drift into irrelevance

All of this finally leads to the drift into irrelevance. If the work of your team can be sourced somewhere else, then people will start doing that. Eventually, a leader high enough up will ask the hard question about what the value of your team really is, or they will simply not understand why your team exists. Once that happens you are doomed to irrelevance, which can soon become redundancy and dismissal.

Influencing to integrate is such an important part of your job as a leader of leaders that you must actively plan it into your work practices.

Don't leave it to chance, and don't leave it until you 'have time'.

It will never happen, and you will be on the slide to irrelevance.

Make influence a planned practice

Influencing to integrate has three components:

- The *perspective*

- The *picture*

- The *practices*

The perspective

The perspective is about how you look at your role and organisation. What do you see as important? What really matters to the organisation achieving its purpose and outcomes? Perspective includes taking a systems view of things and looking for the interconnections, for how one aspect of the organisation feeds into and interacts with another (for example, how workplace culture and values influence customer experience). Taking a systems view will provide a portrait of your organisation that is far more complex than a simple series of linear relationships. Organisations are dynamic, living human communities, and sometimes things happen in the weirdest and most illogical ways!

Your own mood is important in this as well. Working and leading in a mood of curiosity, wonder and possibility further open your perspective.

Another important, but often neglected and even dismissed aspect, is empathy. Empathy is the capacity to put yourself in the shoes of another, and to have a deep understanding of and feeling for the condition of that other. This other can be an individual, a group, a whole society or even the whole world. Empathy is not a soft, flaky feeling, but a practical and motivating capacity of your imagination. Empathy drives powerful, practical and valuable action into the wider world.

Be really interested in the big picture. Don't just live in your own little team bubble.

> Be passionately interested in what is going on with your organisation's strategy, the environment that it is working in, and the shifts going on in the wider world that will have an impact on it.

The picture

If you want to get good at influencing to integrate, you will need a picture that you can keep and update, one that shows all the main interrelationships in your world. This includes relationships with peers, other leaders across the organisation, formal and informal connections, forces at play outside the organisation, emerging trends, and just about anything else you can think of.

A visual is better than a list or a spreadsheet because it can simultaneously show you a range of interconnections. You can create a map with pen and blank (not lined) paper, or you can use various mind-mapping apps. Make sure the app doesn't restrict you to a predefined format that you can't change: you want your map to be as flexible and adaptable as possible to the power and limitless scope of your imagination.

The practices

Armed with your perspective and picture, you are now ready to implement the practices of influencing to integrate.

Step 1: Plan

Book time for influencing to integrate into your calendar for each week and month. How much time you need will depend on your role and the organisation you are in. As a guide, work on spending at least ten per cent or more of your month on influencing to integrate practices. If you are setting up a new role or refreshing an existing role, this may go as high as fifty to sixty per cent.

Step 2: Scan

Scanning is the practice of continually having your curiosity activated as you go through your days and weeks. Be alert to informal conversations, information emails, news items, reports and workshops. Remember, it's called 'scanning' because you don't have to get deep into each of these things: you're just skimming to pick up the essence of what's going on. When you

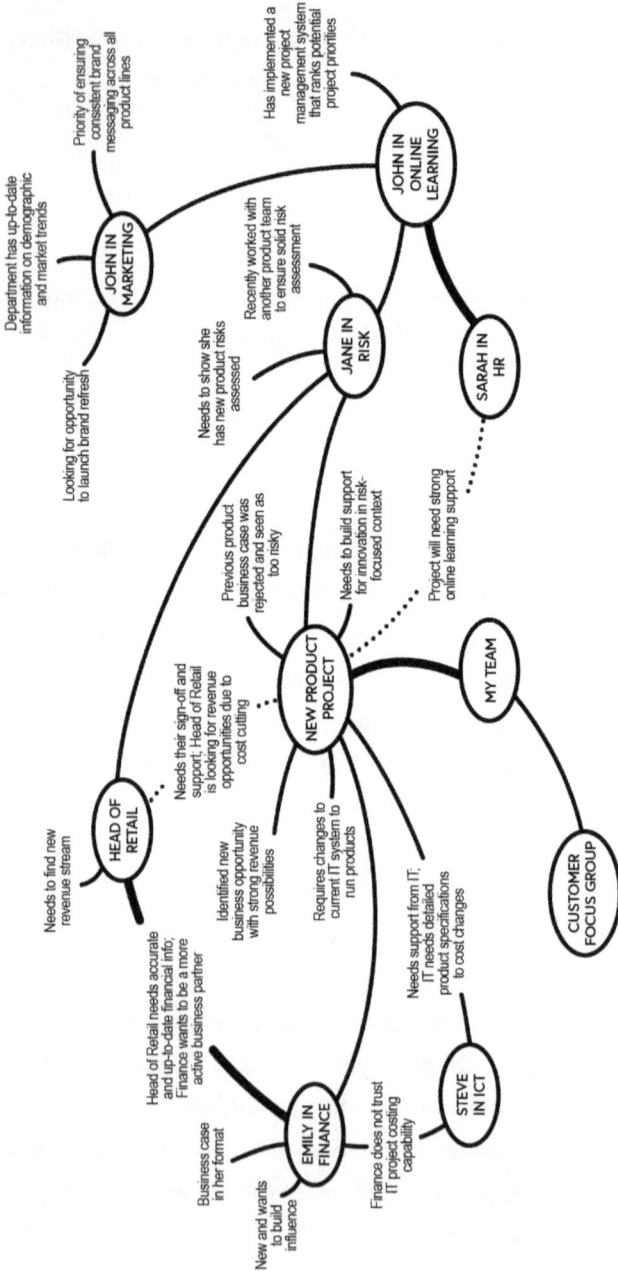

Figure 6. The picture – mapping your key relationships

hit upon something that grabs your attention, you can do a deeper dive then.

What you scan will depend on your role and your organisation. If you are in a government department that looks after agriculture, then you'll likely scan weather trends, global markets for farm goods, and advances in farm technologies. If you work in the lending area of a bank, you will likely scan for shifts in economic conditions, housing market demands, and emerging start-ups in lending.

No matter what field you are in, scanning involves keeping an eye out for all those things that are bigger than your immediate areas of work and responsibility. As a leader of leaders, it's important to stay alert to shifts in internal thinking, strategies, authorities and emerging changes. The best way to do this is to be actively connected.

Step 3: Connect

Make sure you have regular opportunities to connect with the people that your team provides products and services to. These people could be outside your organisation, but more often they will be in another part of the organisation you work in. This is especially true if you work in teams whose job it is to support the effective functioning of the organisation – for example, teams like finance, IT, people and culture, risk, legal, and research and development.

Ideally, these connections and conversations should be face to face. This may not always be possible, but don't just rely on email or messaging. Do all you can to have the opportunity for more open, exploratory, listening-type conversations in which your goal is to listen intently and gain insights and perspectives that you didn't already have.

New leaders of leaders often neglect developing strong, collaborative relationships with their peers. But your peer relationships are vital to your success in your new role. Peers can be a bit like siblings: closely connected and dependent on each other, yet prone to irritating each other from time to time. Often, the work of your teams and the teams of your peers are closely interconnected, so it's important to the organisation and to your own success to build and sustain solid working relationships with your peers. Make sure you get to as many formal and informal gatherings as you can.

Step 4: Educate

You also need to play an important role in continually educating your leaders and your teams about the bigger picture. You want to create teams of scanners – people who are interested in and passionate about how their work sits in the wider environment of the organisation and beyond. It's particularly important to not buy into the idea that you must shelter your team from the harsh realities of the world. In fact, the more you educate them about what's going on in the organisation and beyond, the more they will understand emerging trends and changes.

In a way, it's about treating them like adults, instead of children. People at all levels of an organisation are quite capable of feeling the discomfort of uncertainty while still getting on with their jobs.

> *Engage your team regularly and often in understanding and learning about wider connections and emerging trends. Encourage them to look outside their own role and team.*

Invite your peers or leaders from other parts of the organisation to come and speak to your leaders, or even your whole team, about what is going on in their world. Invite them to speak about their strategy, their current priorities, an exciting project they are running, or some of the tough challenges they face.

The impact of your team

Putting time and effort into influencing to integrate brings a lot of benefits and value to your organisation, your team, and your own success. Doing this allows you to activate the multiplier effect that a great leader of leaders can bring. Here are some of the positive impacts that systematically influencing to integrate can generate:

- You and your team will stay energised and continually open to learning and change. Looking outside of ourselves as individuals, teams and organisations powerfully shifts our perspectives and actions. Nothing drives motivation and engagement more than a clear line between your work and an important service to others.

- You and your team can anticipate and adapt to emerging trends. By developing whole teams of curious scanners, you can see changes on the horizon together. This means you can be better prepared to not only manage change, but also to see and grasp the opportunities in that change as it emerges.

- Emphasising a broader awareness as a natural and regular part of work life means that you, your leaders and your teams can become leaders of innovation in your organisation, either in the work of the team itself or by sharing ideas and insights with other parts of the organisation.

- Your team becomes a leader in the organisation and beyond. Quite often, people who have had the opportunity to work and grow in teams with this external focus and curiosity create opportunities for their expertise and spread passion across the organisation.

- The work of your team will stay relevant, significant and valuable. By keeping alert and alive to the wider environment and influencing to integrate the goals and efforts of your team, you will ensure that your team productively adapts and evolves in an ever-changing world.

By prioritising influencing to integrate, you create clear benefits to both your team and the organisation as a whole.

Over time, it can become one of the most satisfying aspects of your work. It's how lasting legacies are made.

Putting the team on the line

Aisha had a challenge she wasn't quite sure how to process. She had taken on being the leader of her organisation's new people and culture team. Previously, the organisation had never had much more than an industrial relations team to deal with issues with the union, so this was a new initiative as well as a new experience for Aisha.

Aisha knew that it's one thing to set up a new function and hire people into the teams and leader roles, but quite another to actually integrate these teams into the organisation so that the value of what they bring can be realised. So, she scanned for opportunities for her new team. Sure enough, she saw one that was emerging.

The CEO raised the idea of holding a strategy conference for the top hundred leaders in the company. As the idea was discussed, the assumption was that the small strategy team would coordinate the sessions. Aisha immediately saw an important opportunity to activate the value of the learning and development team that was part of her portfolio. She proposed to the CEO that the newly appointed learning and development leader should be given responsibility for designing and running this important three-day conference.

When Aisha told the learning and development leader that he was being given responsibility for the conference, he was initially a bit hesitant. After all, the organisation could be a tough place, and the senior leaders could be critical and difficult to please. But Aisha didn't offer it as a choice: she gave the leader the responsibility as a directive, and off they went!

It was a very intensive six weeks for this leader and his team. They really had to stretch beyond what they were comfortable with, and had to engage the time and resources of teams across the organisation. They knew that the conference had to be a highly engaging, meaningful and well-executed experience.

There were a few crucial moments in the conference that could have gone either way, but overall, the conference was a great success and proved to be a catalyst for organisational change. It really served to put both the learning and development team and the entire people and culture group on the organisational map. This led to a whole range of important people-and-culture initiatives across the organisation, which achieved important outcomes for the business.

By scanning and seizing on this opportunity, Aisha successfully influenced to integrate. She put one of her teams right on the line, and, as a result, the organisation was able to gain the full value of a function that was important to the future of the business.

IDEAS FOR ACTION

1. Create a picture of the ecosystem that you and your teams operate in.

2. Identify the team's current important relationships, and the relationships that are emerging as important for the future.

3. Based on this picture, create a list of the top five actions you will take to influence those relationships.

4. Set up regular catch-ups with the top three people you will need to influence. These catch-ups are about you listening to and understanding the opportunities and concerns that these people are facing.

QUESTIONS TO DIG DEEPER

1. How would you assess the status of your influencing-to-integrate activities?

2. What mood do you find yourself in when you think about influencing to integrate? How might this mood affect the actions you will take?

3. What opportunities can you imagine for your team, your organisation, and the world if you more actively influenced to integrate?

Your new future

Transitions are getting faster and faster

JANICE TRAINED AS A PHYSIOTHERAPIST. OVER THE COURSE of her career, she worked in a wide range of clinical roles in both public hospitals and private practices. She was a conscientious, caring and hard-working physio who treated all kinds of clients, from homeless people to sports stars and politicians. Over the years, Janice also found herself in head physio roles managing physiotherapy departments in hospitals, while continuing to manage her own patient list as well.

Janice had never really considered stepping out of the profession she trained in, until she was identified as a high-potential leader in her organisation's talent management program. Janice ended up jumping in the deep end with more demanding roles: she was operations manager at a regional hospital for a time, and then also quality manager. These roles were completely differ-ent from her clinical work, and while they had a steep learning curve and were at times overwhelming, Janice began to enjoy the stimulation of learning new jobs. Most recently, Janice won the job of manager of allied health in a major teaching hospital in the city, a full-blown leader-of-leaders role in which nine team managers report to her across a wide range of health specialties.

As you can see, Janice has successfully navigated the challenging yet rewarding road of becoming a leader of leaders. Now, she leads other leaders who manage teams of clinical experts outside of her own original profession, and she is influencing across the hospital's executive team in a major redevelopment of this large hospital.

Here's the thing: the rapid transitions that Janice experienced all happened over a two-year period. As the world moves faster, leadership transitions are becoming faster and more frequent.

This is a big transition

The transition from team leader to leader of leaders is a story of profound growth and change. This new role is such a different job from being a team leader, and is pretty much a whole different life compared to your days as a professional contributor. The stakes are high for you, the team and the organisation, and many of the ways of thinking and working that made you a successful team leader are now your greatest risks.

Unlearning old ways that have served you well in the past is difficult. What makes this really challenging is that you have learned so well! You have so internalised how you do things that you can't easily see what these mindsets and practices are. But that's the great gift in the overwork, confusion, and sense of being lost that you will likely encounter when you begin your new role: these are the messages that are telling you that your tried-and-true methods are no longer cutting it. Your feeling of overwhelm is leading you towards change.

The way ahead brings expanded possibilities

This transition to leader of leaders holds many different experiences, challenges and changes. We have seen that there are four phases to this process, which basically work from the inside out. At the core is the idea of your way-of-being, and the essential practice of observing your way-of-being day-to-day in your work. You can do this through noticing the language you use when speaking to yourself, and to others. You can also pay more attention to your emotions and moods, because they are windows into your inner world of beliefs and assessments. The one that is the quickest to access in the moment is the shifts in your own body: your acture and bodily reactions are physical manifestations of how you are currently interpreting your experience.

You will act in the world according to how you see yourself in the world. Committing to the practice of 'giving yourself the promotion' will accelerate your move into your new role. Change your rituals, ceremonies, look, feel and language to uniquely shift how you see yourself in the world.

This lays the foundation for the two big changes in your leadership practices. The first is constructing sandboxes for your leaders, consciously designing the space in which your team leaders can thrive and construct high-performing teams. These will also become the places where emerging leaders get to practice and grow as real leaders.

The second big change in your leadership practices is influencing to integrate the work of your teams into the wider organisation. As your team leaders lead and ensure the work of your teams gets done, you will have the time and mental space to influence the organisation and ensure the purpose and work of your teams stays relevant, vibrant and innovative. You open yourself up to bigger and wider possibilities for positive impact in the world, and also open your leaders and teams up to the realities of the environment they are in so that they can continually grow and adapt.

Now more than ever, our world needs great leaders of leaders. As you establish yourself in this role, you will release more brilliance and energy into the world to solve the big problems and create the new future.

Coaching real people to be real leaders of leaders

The four phases in the journey to become a leader of leaders have been forged through working with hundreds of people like you, who have found themselves thrust into big roles that felt beyond their abilities and stamina. The experiences of these people were profound, and the impact of this struggle on them, their careers, their relationships, their health and their lives was stressful and, at times, even shattering. Simple techniques and motivational talks were useless. They needed change more than anything. This transition is deep, and must be at the core of your being for you to sustain the energy and focus required to be a leader of leaders.

The approaches in this book were generated through my study of organisational life, leadership, and what it is to be human. The essential human qualities of openness, vulnerability and brilliance are at the core of my practices. One of the most powerful insights I have gained through working with leaders is that each one of us is a unique being. Yes, we can learn from collective experience and wisdom, but when it gets down to it, we must find the way that works for us.

The exciting thing about working as a leadership coach and in so many different roles and organisations is that I know it is possible for you to become the unique leader of leaders that only you can be. I would love the opportunity to work with you and walk with you on your own journey of growth and change to become a great leader of leaders. You have more positive impact to bring into the world.

Connect with me

As an author and leadership coach I specialise in helping professional contributors and team leaders grow into successful senior leaders. I have helped hundreds of people make this important and profound transition. Many of these people have gone on to even bigger leadership roles, and have expanded their positive impact in the world beyond what they ever imagined.

It is with great pride that *Becoming a Leader of Leaders* has been used as the foundation for the leadership development program designed and delivered by Being Leaders. Being Leaders is where people transform from overworked to incredibly impactful. The practical tools and resources offered through the Being Leaders program are designed to make an immediate impact for people in leader-of-leaders roles.

The Sandbox Triangle® and The Sandbox Triangle® graphic are now registered trademarks in Australia of Being Leaders Pty Ltd.

To connect with the team at Being Leaders, visit their website at www.beingleaders.com.au or via email at info@beingleaders.com.au.

Acknowledgements

Where do you get your ideas from? How do we know the stuff we know? As I look back over the ideas and practices covered in this book, some of them have a clear origin, while others bring forth a sea of faces in my mind from the wide range of people whom I have known, worked with and talked to over the years.

The wonderful thing about being a coach and leadership facilitator is that every day I learn from the people I work with. The ideas and practices in this book have all been refined and tested in shaping real leadership work in real organisations by the wonderful people I have worked with. They are people in different roles and from different organisations, and most of them probably think of themselves as ordinary people doing a job, living their life, enjoying their joys and enduring their pains. But none of them are ordinary. *No* human being is ordinary. I want to acknowledge the wisdom, insight and straight-out courage of the people I have had the honour to work with. Not all of them were in jobs that they loved or that were necessarily their ideal career, but they kept showing up and putting themselves out into the world every day to get important things done for other people.

There are other ideas and practices that have a much clearer origin. The most significant is Alan Sieler from the Newfield Institute in Melbourne, Australia. In 2014, I enrolled in the institute's graduate diploma program of Ontological Coaching. This intensive, eighteen-month course of study changed my professional and personal life. Through the application of the ideas of ontological coaching and way-of-being, I have seen rapid, profound and lasting change in the effectiveness of leadership transitions. Thank you to Alan for his grounded humility and deep wisdom. I also want to acknowledge Paula Drayton and Tony Carew from Liberated Leaders, for their generosity in sharing their program and the wisdom emerging from the ontological coaching field.

My greatest privilege has been to observe and be involved in the experiences and growth of my family and their contributions to the world. My wife, a health manager in a large, busy major hospital who faces the complexity of leading other leaders every day, and who has a reputation as a leader who drives important outcomes in the health system in a human and loving way. My eldest daughter, to whom this book is dedicated, who brought the voices of others to life in her writing and performances as a comedian and actor, and especially in her one-woman show, *Temporary*. My second daughter, who is making the demanding journey from accountant to senior executive, and who is constantly staying open to learning and change. My eldest son, a sports management leader and entrepreneur, who imagines possibilities and then gets on with bringing them to life while gaining and sustaining the respect of many. My youngest son, a software engineer and one of the best listeners I have ever met, who is capable of naturally facilitating conversations and who gently but firmly continues to lead me towards new ways of seeing. To all of you – thank you.

And thank you to all the people who remind me every day of just how incredible human beings and humanity can be when we apply our strengths and skills to create the best possible future.

Further reading

Coaching to the Human Soul – Alan Sieler, available from the Newfield Institute website

Your Body is Your Brain – Amanda Blake, Trokay Press 2018

The Tree of Knowledge – Humberto R. Maturana and Francisco J. Varela, Shambala 1998

www.ingramcontent.com/pod-product-compliance
Lightning Source LLC
Chambersburg PA
CBHW031855200326
41597CB00012B/424